BEAUTIFUL CHURCHES

FRANCES LINCOLN LIMITED
PUBLISHERS

BEAUTIFUL CHURCHES

SAVED BY THE CHURCHES CONSERVATION TRUST

MATTHEW BYRNE

FOREWORD BY HRH THE PRINCE OF WALES

Members of the St Paul family at Snarford, Lincolnshire. Their strangely rigid attitudes and the use of multi-coloured marbles are typical of the early seventeenth century.

Beautiful Churches
Frances Lincoln Ltd
74–77 White Lion Street, London N1 9PF
www.franceslincoln.com

ISBN: 978-0-7112-3453-6 (hardback)
ISBN: 978-0-7112-3456-7 (paperback)

Printed and bound in China

9 8 7 6 5 4 3 2 1

THE CHURCHES
CONSERVATION TRUST

CONTENTS

FOREWORD

HRH THE PRINCE OF WALES

CLARENCE HOUSE

As President of The Churches Conservation Trust, it gives me great pleasure to introduce this book, 'Beautiful Churches', to you. I have particularly enjoyed visiting many of the churches under the protection of the Trust over the years and on every occasion I marvel at the beauty and history which each contains. These churches are a defining feature of the English landscape and of the towns and villages which they serve. It is of the utmost importance to ensure that they are protected for future generations to enjoy.

In this book, Matthew Byrne takes us on a journey to thirty-six special churches from The Churches Conservation Trust's wonderful collection. It is not easy to pick out the best from such a treasure-trove, but I hope you might agree that his book provides an enthralling journey through some of the highlights of English church architecture.

I have the greatest admiration for the work of the Trust and all the volunteers who so faithfully devote themselves to opening these churches to the public. I can only urge you to support their marvellous efforts to encourage more people to understand, enjoy and support our ecclesiastical heritage. They have been conserving these great buildings for over forty years and have helped to put many back at the heart of local community life.

These thirty-six churches are just a sample of over 340 that the Trust cares for across the country. Each is unique in its own way and a visit is always richly rewarding.

PREFACE

SARAH ROBINSON, DEPUTY CHIEF EXECUTIVE
AND DIRECTOR OF CONSERVATION,
CHURCHES CONSERVATION TRUST

THE CHURCHES CONSERVATION TRUST is proud to have played such an important role in national life for over forty years, protecting more than 340 wonderful historic buildings that might otherwise have disappeared altogether. Today, the churches in our care form one of the world's greatest collections of ecclesiastical architecture and art.

The Trust's story began in the 1960s, a difficult period for historic churches. Many were falling into disrepair and some faced the very real threat of demolition. If it had not been for the commitment of local communities and national campaigners, many of the historic churches we know and love today might have been lost. It was also thanks to the tireless campaigning of church enthusiasts that our organisation came into being – originally as the Redundant Churches Fund, a unique partnership between the Church, State and Charity sectors.

The first church to be saved was the Grade I medieval St Peter's Edlington, which had had its roof and windows removed in an attempt to turn it into a ruin. St Peter's was in a disadvantaged area in the coalfields of South Yorkshire and with no organisation able to take on redundant but important historic churches, and no appetite for demolition, St Peter's had been left victim to the ravages of the weather and vandalism. Furnishings had been removed to nearby churches and the door locked for apparently the last time. Thanks to the timely intervention of the new national charity, it is now a highly valued community and arts building, regularly used by local schools and colleges.

In 1994, we celebrated our 25th anniversary, and adopted our new name – the Churches Conservation Trust – to reflect the evolving nature of our work, especially the focus on bringing our churches back into community use.

Repair and conservation work at St Mary's Church, Redgrave, Suffolk, a vast country church set in open fields.

A number of our achievements over the years, both in the conservation and new use of churches, have won national and international awards. All our churches are listed, mostly Grade I, and some are Scheduled Ancient Monuments. Each one remains consecrated and a few may even return to parish use.

The reasons for protecting them differ enormously, but all revolve around a real historic, architectural or cultural significance. Some provide unexpected delights to discover on a country walk, others offer a place for people to get together, or for personal reflection.

Many projects and events take place in CCT churches as part of their exciting uses for tourism, volunteering, education, arts and the community. Our work includes undertaking over fifty specialist conservation repair projects every year and many more minor repairs. As a charity, we rely heavily on the support of volunteers and donations to help us achieve our aims.

All of the churches highlighted in this book have been carefully and often extensively repaired by the Trust.

Our repair philosophy follows closely the principles laid down by William Morris in his manifesto for the Society for the Protection of Ancient Buildings, with its emphasis on repair rather than replacement, protection rather than restoration, good maintenance and housekeeping to withstand the effects of decay, and respect for the changes that each new generation has proudly brought to these buildings. The marks of a medieval plasterer may look rough but they confront us directly with the hands of a craftsman working 500 years ago. Eleventh-century stonework may now be worn and untidy but that surface has been there since William the Conqueror and is irreplaceable. A Victorian stove may clutter an ancient nave, but it is part of the story of the church and those who have used it.

Each programme of work is carefully thought through so only that which is necessary is undertaken, not just because this is cost effective, but because the principle has proved over time to be the best for the buildings we care for. The greatest

compliment to the Trust would be for visitors before and after our repair work to notice little difference, except a feeling that the church seems more welcoming . . . and, in some cases, drier!

Repairs undertaken to St Margaret of Antioch, Knotting, near Bedford, a recent addition to our estate, illustrate how our philosophy is put into practice. The oldest part of St Margaret's is mid-twelfth century, although it is conjecture that the tower arch might be earlier. The church was remodelled in the Gothic style in the fourteenth and fifteenth centuries and then again, rather unusually for a rural church, in the seventeenth century. It has a charming light-filled interior with mainly seventeenth-century fittings, one of the most interesting features of which is the Laudian gates separating chancel from nave, apparently erected by Archbishop Laud in order to put a stop to the locals holding cockfights. St Margaret's was in a poor state when transferred to the Trust, mainly due to damp ingress and the use of modern and inappropriate materials in the late twentieth century.

Our first priority was to replace broken roof tiles that were

allowing water to get in. A concrete channel had also cracked sufficiently to ensure a ready supply of rainwater into the base of the church walls, so this was taken up and replaced with an efficient ground drain. Hard cement pointing was removed where loose and repointed in lime mortar. In places where stonework had decayed so badly that replacement was necessary, we decided to continue with the brick slip and tile repairs made in the 1920s by the renowned architect Albert Richardson, thus continuing a change in repair philosophy made in the last century.

Inside, decayed pew platforms and spongy chipboard tower floors were replaced with oak, and rush matting behind wall benches was retained and brushed down, but the biggest challenge was the interior decoration. A relatively recently applied hard white wall covering had failed dramatically and was peeling off the walls in patches. A sensitive, though very time-consuming process of removal was successfully deployed.

Gradually, the harsh white finish gave way to reveal beautiful layers of salmon-pink limewash, in varying degrees of colour and intensity. The end result is a place where visitors can enjoy discovering the richness of our church heritage.

FAR LEFT *Conservation of painted panels by Wyndham Hope Hughes on the the pulpit at All Saints' Church, Cambridge, designed by G.F.Bodley.*

LEFT *Conservation of an original Norman doorway at the Church of St Mary the Virgin, Little Hormead, Hertfordshire.*

RIGHT *Conservation of the carved pews at St John the Evangelist, the oldest church in Leeds city centre.*

While most of our funds are spent on keeping churches wind- and water-tight, occasionally we have the opportunity to work on wonderful rare treasures.

An imposing old oak door at the quiet church of St Mary, Little Hormead dates to between 1130 and 1150 and is one of the earliest in England. The gnarled oak door covered in weathered decorative iron strapwork – bold geometrical scroll and dragon designs – used to sit in the north entrance to the church until Victorian times, when it was moved inside for display. It is of national, possibly international significance and has been compared to the elegant doors of Durham Cathedral.

St Mary's was vested in 1997, and by 2010 we were concerned about the condition of both timber and ironwork. Investigation concluded that the door had been repaired a few times during its life. At some point a threshold stone had been inserted in the doorway, probably to keep back the rising churchyard ground, and this had led to decay of the bottom timber panels. These had been backed by oak strips in the eighteenth century. A badly detailed oak frame had been nailed on to the back of the door in 1903, and at some point all the timber had been coated

in resin. Minimal intervention was only a consideration if the front of the door could be protected – the ironwork was also fragile, and while we could re-attach it using original nail holes, the decorative dragons would not be immune from determined efforts to remove them.

After much soul searching, the 1903 oak backing frame was removed; voids in the panels were filled in using carefully shaped oak inserts; splinters caused by the 1903 nails were trimmed and refixed using animal glue; the ironwork was sensitively fixed back into position and the whole door given a coating of microcrystalline wax. Protection is given by a non-reflective glass panel so that this extraordinary example of medieval craftsmanship can be seen by those who visit this unassuming church.

While conservation remains at the heart of what the Trust does, over the past ten years we have realised that these buildings should not just be monuments to the past but also part of our lives today, as places for the community, tourist attractions and, in some cases, put to alternative uses. Above all, though, they are places of discovery and delight.

INTRODUCTION

M Y FIRST TWO VISITS TO CHURCHES cared for by the Churches Conservation Trust, then known as the Redundant Churches Fund (Preface), were in 1982 at Little Washbourne, Gloucestershire (pages 148–51) and Theddlethorpe All Saints, Lincolnshire (pages 64–8). They differ in several ways. Washbourne is alone in an old apple orchard beneath the western escarpment of the Cotswolds; Theddlethorpe is in the north Lincolnshire marshland that borders the coast, a landscape as flat as any can be, with just two large houses as neighbours. Washbourne is a small towerless church of nave and chancel only; Theddlethorpe is a large aisled building mostly of the late Middle Ages. Although it is much the older, Washbourne was refaced with smoothly cut golden limestone in the eighteenth century; Theddlethorpe is a remarkable mixture of weathered green sandstone, limestone and brick, a much more rustic effect. The interior of Washbourne clearly shows its Norman origins, raw and powerful, but every square foot is filled with remarkably swagger eighteenth century box pews. Much of the interior of Theddlethorpe is now free of benches giving an unusual sense of space that emphasises the role of the arcades that separate nave and aisles. Although there is much fine carving in wood and stone the effect inside, like that outside, is rustic rather than grand. Despite all these differences the two churches are strikingly similar in overall character. Most village churches are surrounded by houses; these two are not as remote as several of the churches described in the following pages but they stand in relative isolation like free spirits in an overcrowded world. The external and internal fabric of both is well cared for without being robbed of the attractively mellow appearance of old age by over-zealous maintenance. Most memorably, the interiors exude the undisturbed atmosphere of past ages,

which reflects the history and attitudes of village people who have worshipped here for countless generations.

Visits to over a hundred Trust churches followed after 1982 and it became apparent that despite a wide diversity of ages and architectural styles their often isolated situations and special atmospheres gave them a recognisable character of their own. Most of the visits were made with a camera and the resulting photographs confirmed the impression of churches which in some important respects had a common corporate personality arising from their past history and present circumstances in the care of the same organisation and it seemed that this might form the basis of a book. A good deal of travelling and photography eventually made the idea a reality. It was clear that the book should be sufficiently pictorial to illustrate the architecture and furnishings of the churches in all their variety – the sumptuously fine and the endearingly simple. A book on churches should also attempt to explain the invisibles that lie behind the visibles and which made the latter what they are. Churches are meeting places of the divine spirit with human beings and the buildings and their furnishings in their present forms are the result of changing human beliefs and attitudes in several spheres: religious, political, social, emotional and artistic. A knowledge of why, how and when this happened is likely to help in the understanding and enjoyment of what is seen in the architecture and art of churches today.

It was always envisaged that the book would be a tribute to and in some small way a means of publicising the work of the Churches Conservation Trust without which some hundreds of churches might now be ruinous or put to inappropriate use. It is work that deserves to be brought to the

Trust churches are frequently off-road, remote from any habitation. The one at Pendock, Worcestershire, is approached by a cart track across a field. The site of a deserted village lies to its left.

attention of a wide public.

The Trust has churches in such mainly modern cities as Liverpool and Leeds, in smaller cities such as Gloucester, Cambridge and York and in market towns like Shrewsbury and Evesham, but these are not typical Trust territory. Most of its churches are situated in places where the enjoyment of visiting them involves the additional enjoyment of journeys to immensely secret places hidden within some of most beautiful and spectacular regions of England. Trust churches are to be found in small isolated villages or quite alone at the ends of long country lanes or among fields reached only by footpaths or hidden inside the parks of stately houses. This is no surprise or coincidence because the churches handed over to the care of the Trust have ceased to be required for parochial use by the Church of England because the congregations needed to support them and their clergy are too small. Some villages disappeared completely in the Middle Ages due to outbreaks of plague, frequent flooding, the clearance of land for sheep farming and other causes, and this has left the parish church, now in the Trust's care, as a solitary remnant of a once thriving community. The existence of several Trust churches alone inside the parks of stately houses is witness to the peremptory banishment of the villages they once served to a place beyond the lordly domain in the eighteenth century. A few examples will suffice to illustrate the sort of places that visitors to Trust churches will see.

The last leg of the journey to St Ninian's church (Ninekirks), Brougham, Cumbria, starts from the Penrith to Appleby road which crosses the wide open landscape north of the Lake District where there is a distant view of the long line of the Pennine hills if travelling east or of the Cumbrian mountains if travelling west. Only those looking for it will spot an inconspicuous wooden signpost by a gate indicating the way to Ninekirks on foot. The footpath follows the River Eamont for half a mile above its high sandstone banks which glow red on a sunny day. The path tops a crest and

rounds a corner to reveal a low towerless church a few hundred yards away. Built by a redoubtable seventeenth-century countess it stands totally and mysteriously alone in a circular churchyard in the middle of a field (pages 83–7).

In the south-west of England the Roseland Peninsula is one of the remotest on the south Cornish coast. The last few miles to the end of the peninsula are a narrow, often single lane road which eventually runs steeply downhill and ends abruptly at a little quayside on a small creek which is a side-branch of a larger creek which stretches several miles inland from St Mawes Head. The immediate surprise in this lonely place is the extensive lawn which runs up from the quay to the long towered frontage of a nineteenth-century neo-Gothic mansion. The small spire of a church behind peeps above the roof line of the house (page 50). Apart from two estate cottages buried away in trees there are no other buildings. The church is reached by returning a few hundred yards back up the road, crossing a stile and following a footpath beneath a canopy of tall trees. At the time of my visits in April, a bright splash of red was provided by camellia bushes in full flower. The little church has a fine Norman south doorway and its north transept is actually attached to the rear of the big house. This is the church of St Anthony-in-Roseland, perhaps the most beguiling dedication in England. The history of the church is a fascinating one. Despite its isolation the church attracts a steady trickle of visitors because the adjacent path around the peninsula is a favourite with hikers who call in for a few minutes.

The historic market town of Ludlow in Shropshire is one of the architectural gems of England. A few miles to the south the main road to Hereford by-passes a steep hill which can be ascended by a minor road. This leads to the top where there are splendid views across the whole of Herefordshire to the Black Mountains in the south. The broad hilltop is the site of Richards Castle and its eponymous village. What remains up here is a

(page 139).

(page 15).

Painted rood screens were defaced or removed from most medieval churches during the Reformation or in Victorian restorations. The one at Strensham, Worcestershire, was re-reused as the front of a west gallery. This detail shows four of the long line of twenty-three saints and their identifying symbols. Left to right: St Erasmus (with windlass), St Lawrence (with gridiron), St Stephen (with stones), St Antony (with pig).

microcosm of early English history. The modern village has understandably migrated to the bottom of the hill leaving only a few cottages, the large early medieval church of St Bartholomew and the ruins of the Norman castle. This was one of several which guarded the militarily strategic border between England and Wales. The ruins are not of the carefully tidied up sort surrounded by manicured lawns. To see it now involves penetrating the enveloping trees and shrubs. The long broad nave of the church is crammed with eighteenth-century box pews, enough of them to seat several hundred people, an extraordinary congregation given the remoteness and the arduous climb on foot or

horseback at the time the pews were installed (page 139).

The Trust has several churches hidden within the parks of stately houses as already mentioned. At Gunton not far from the north-east Norfolk coast there is no sign of a church in the village. A long high wall with woodland beyond suggests a park and house of aristocracy. The park is entered through tall gateposts with lodges on either side and a winding driveway leads some way in front of a large eighteenth-century house. A little further on, vehicles must be parked where the drive gives way to a path leading into a wood. After a short walk the path leads into a little clearing where the house is just visible to the left between the trees. To the right, facing the house, is a giant Classical temple portico which is actually the parish church of St Andrew (page 104). It would be a handsome if unremarkable building on the high street of a market town or in a square in the Georgian quarter of a large city but here inside a wood inside a park in rural Norfolk it is an extraordinary sight, the more so since it is encountered so unexpectedly. The church was designed in 1769 by the famous Neoclassical architect Robert Adam.

These four churches and many more like them in the Trust's care are places of perfect solitude and silence, where the visitor might not meet another in a whole day. For those who love the combination of ancient architecture and landscape they are magical places.

Every period of church building in England with its associated architectural style is represented in Trust churches: Anglo Saxon, Norman, medieval Gothic, seventeenth and eighteenth century Classical and Victorian Gothic Revival. There are large and small churches, grand and humble churches. In architecture size and quality are not necessarily related any more than they are in, say, painting or sculpture. The large church and detached bell tower at West Walton, Norfolk (pages 44–9) are examples of the finest pieces of thirteenth-century Early English Gothic architecture in England and the equally large large churches at Theddlethorpe All Saints, Lincolnshire (pages 64–8) are excellent examples of the later Perpendicular Gothic period. By contrast the big churches at Wiggenhall, Norfolk (pages 76–9) and Richards Castle, Shropshire (pages 137–40) are relatively plain. The two small neighbouring churches at Hales and Heckingham, Norfolk (pages 32–4) have splendidly ornate and interesting Norman architecture whereas the equally small churches at Winterborne Tomson, Dorset (pages 29–31) and Lead, West Yorkshire (pages 132–4) have the plainest of exteriors but interesting interiors. On the whole Trust churches tend to be small

because they served communities that were always small and are often smaller now.

The size of a church and its external architecture are, however, no guide to the furnishings inside, such as stained glass, monuments, fonts and woodwork in the form of roofs, screens and benches. A church that was built very plainly in the early Middle Ages may have acquired many fine examples of these things at a later time. Even in a very poor parish it only required one or two people to provide the necessary finance. It might be a wealthy pious parishioner or a local boy made good as an archbishop, bishop or abbot who wished to be remembered on his home patch. This is why many Trust churches are more interesting inside than outside. The tiny Withcote Chapel, Leicestershire, (pages 80–2), has an almost complete set of good late medieval stained glass made by Henry VIII's glazier. Innumerable churches have glass by the leading Victorian artists including William Morris and Edward Burne-Jones. The church at Wiggenhall St Mary the Virgin, Norfolk has one of the finest sets of elaborately carved medieval benches in England (page 77). Small Classical churches built in the eighteenth century have elegant woodwork of the period when imported woods like mahogany sometimes inlaid with other woods have replaced English oak. There are good examples at Gunton, Norfolk (pages 104–7) and Chiselhampton, Oxfordshire (pages 96–9).

No group of people has transformed the interiors of churches, including small rural churches, more than the successive generations of wealthy aristocratic families living in the big houses in the surrounding parishes. Whatever their prominence in national affairs these people regarded their ancestral country seats as their true homes and their own parish churches, however humble, as their resting places. Monuments that made a conspicuous display of the family's wealth and status were important from the earliest times but ambitions increased steadily during the Middle

Two funeral hatchments at Edmonthorpe, Leicestershire. These family armorial banners were used at funerals of the aristocracy in the eighteenth and early nineteenth centuries, and later hung in the church. Removed from many churches during Victorian restorations, they are common in Trust churches.

Ages and the Elizabethan, Jacobean and Georgian periods leading to ever larger and more grandiose creations, They provide fascinating insights into styles of art, fashions in dress and particularly into the social attitudes of their times. Medieval effigies lie serenely on simple table tombs their hands piously joined in prayer, as at Allerton Mauleverer, here unusually carved in wood (page 21). After 1550 the designs became more varied. The effigies could remain on simple table tombs, as at Holme Lacy, Herefordshire (page 143), or they could rise to a kneeling position or appear as busts in niches. The recumbent effigies could be surrounded by Classical four-poster canopies large enough to reach into the rafters of a small church. They are often now the most colourful things in a church, a riot of gilding and bright colours, such as those at Snarford, Lincolnshire (see Contents page). From the early seventeenth century, imported marbles were popular, white for the the figures and black for the surrounds, as at Croome d'Abitot, Worcestershire (pages 118–19). In the seventeenth and throughout the eighteenth century, the effigies sat, lounged on couches or rose erect in swagger, gesticulating poses, lords of all they surveyed within their parish domains. There are good examples at Stapleford, Leicestershire (page 127), Strensham, Worcestershire (page 22), Croome d'Abitot and Holme Lacy (*ibid.*). From the beginning of the nineteenth century, monuments became more sentimental, showing grieving widows and widowers and the deathbeds of infant children with attendant angels. Holme Lacy and Nuneham Courtenay, Oxfordshire (page 112) have typical examples. At all periods the leading sculptors of the day were employed. The sculptors of the monuments in the places quoted include Nicholas Stone in the early seventeenth century, Grinling Gibbons in the late seventeenth century (he worked in stone as well as wood) and John Michael Rysbrack in the eighteenth century, men whose works appear in Westminster Abbey and St Paul's Cathedral, London. Over the centuries a

small church could become so crowded with these monuments in chancels, transepts and naves that there is now scarcely room for the living. It is an eerie reminder of human mortality to wander among them in lonely silence in a Trust church, within inches of the greatest sculptural art in England, stared at by the eyes of aristocratic ghosts.

Objects associated with monuments that are often seen in churches are funeral hatchments. These are paintings of the arms of the deceased on canvas or wood which were hung on the façade of a big house before a funeral and transferred to

Fine stained glass in Trust churches ranges from medieval to late Victorian. Left: A detail of the vast east window at St Mary's, Shrewsbury, made in c.1350, shows Old Testament prophets above and the donor of the window, Sir John de Charleton and his sons below. Right: Some of the unusually fine Victorian glass at Bywell, Northumberland. It dates from the 1880s and shows Old Testament figures.

the walls of the parish church thereafter. They were often removed from churches in the late Victorian period but Trust churches have large numbers of them such as those at Edmondthorpe, Leicestershire (page 17). It requires some expertise in heraldry to read the story they tell.

One type of furnishing that is common in Trust churches but is now rare elsewhere is the furnishing connected with preaching in the seventeenth, eighteenth and early nineteenth centuries, not only the pulpits for the clergy but also the pews for the congregations. Their presence

in either a large or small church can dominate the whole interior, such as at Holy Trinity, York (page 63), Fylingdales, North Yorkshire (pages 156–7) and Old Dilton, Wiltshire (page 136). Before the Reformation, the main service in any church was the celebration of the mass or eucharist. The focus of the celebration was the priest in the chancel separated from people in the nave by a tall rood screen. Sermons were preached during the mass although the rural clergy were seldom more educated than the laity and the emphasis was on the reception of Holy Communion. Seating was not always provided for the congregation. After the Reformation, the preaching of the Word (the Bible) was regarded as more important than the Sacrament (the eucharist). From the seventeenth century onwards, the Anglican clergy were scholarly and educated men, graduates of Oxford or Cambridge universities, who were trained in theology and scripture. They regarded preaching as their principal duty so that sermons could last for up to an hour within the services of matins and evensong on Sundays. Such preaching was valuable in principle although it is doubtful whether the learned and rather arid theology the clergy preached was of great use to uneducated agricultural workers. Celebration of the Sacrament could take place as little as four times a year in the average parish church. Whatever the service, the externals of worship were dignified and restrained compared with the colourful drama of Catholic services. As a result of these new attitudes, the most prominent feature of a pre-Reformation church, the altar and associated furnishings in the chancel such as sedilia (seats) for the clergy and piscinae (for the washing of communion vessels) became largely redundant. Stone altars were replaced by simple wooden 'holy tables'. Pre-eminence was now given to the place of preaching. Tall three-decker pulpits enabled the preacher to be seen and heard by the congregation. The bottom deck was for the parish clerk who led the responses to the prayers; the middle deck was where the preacher read the lessons; the top deck was where he preached his sermon. The sound of his voice was focussed by a tester above. There are many examples illustrated. In very 'low' churches the pulpit might be placed centrally in front of the small altar table which was then invisible from the nave, as at Chichester (page 153). Simpler, older benches were removed and every inch of floor space was filled with box pews with seats on one, two or three sides. These enclosures had the practical advantage of shielding the people from the draughts in unheated churches before the advent of Victorian central heating systems. The box pews give an insight into the social attitudes of the time. The box pews of gentry and the wealthier farmers were taller and more spacious at the front of the church; family names would be elegantly inscribed on brass door plates and a substantial annual pew rent would be paid for exclusive use of the pew. The pews further back for tradesmen and artisans would be lower. Labourers and the like might have simple benches at the back or in a west gallery. If the parish contained the seat of a duke, viscount or earl, the family would be hidden from the public gaze in a transept or a special box or gallery, often equipped with its own fireplace as at Stapleford, Leicestershire (page 126). When these furnishings were inserted into an existing medieval church, they were usually made of native English oak. In contemporary eighteenth-century churches they could be made from imported mahogany with inlaid woods and richly ornate carving for the pulpit. A similarly sumptuous reredos was often placed behind the altar inscribed with the Commandments, Creed and Lord's Prayer. The display of the Royal Arms had been obligatory since the time of Elizabeth I to emphasise the sovereign as Supreme Governor of the Church of England. Most existing examples date from the Restoration in 1660 to the beginning of the nineteenth century. Few were set up for Queen Victoria in 1837 and many former arms were taken down later in the century during restorations. However, many survive in Trust churches such as Stourmouth, Kent (page 60). At the time that box pews were inserted, the older earthenware floors were covered with handsome stone flags, which give a building considerable character. For reasons given below, most box pews and three-decker pulpits were swept away from the late nineteenth century onwards. A large proportion of the surviving characteristic interiors of these 'preaching' or 'auditory' churches are now in the care of the Trust.

In the early part of the nineteenth century many clergy of the Church of England were concerned that the nation was falling into religious apathy, indicated by decreasing church attendance. From the 1830s onwards, the High Church Oxford Movement attempted to create a revival of faith by emphasising the Catholic roots of the Church of England before the Reformation. Theologically this meant a greater emphasis on the celebration of the Sacrament as opposed to the preaching of the Word. Architecturally, a return to the spirituality of the Middle Ages meant a return to Gothic architecture. At an early stage A.W.N. Pugin and John Ruskin were passionate advocates of a Gothic Revival. In Pugin's case it was not simply a taste in architectural style. He was a convert to Roman Catholicism who believed that the only architecture appropriate for a Christian church was the Gothic of the Catholic Middle Ages and that Christian architecture based on the pagan temples of ancient Greece and Rome was an abhorence. The Evangelical wing of the Church of England was deeply suspicious of any theology that they regarded as a return to 'popery' but by the latter part of nineteenth century there was a widespread acceptance of many of the ideals of the Oxford Movement. Leading architects quickly followed Pugin and Ruskin in a preference for Gothic architecture in both church and secular buildings. The religious revival of the nineteenth century led to the building of some 6,000 churches in Victoria's reign, mainly in the expanding suburbs of cities

and towns. The great majority were in the new Gothic Revival style, with a special preference for the Decorated, or 'Middle Pointed', Gothic. Some of the finest churches were built by the private benefactions of wealthy landowners and clergy, sometimes in cities, sometimes in remote places. An example of the latter in the Trust's care is at Skelton-cum-Newby, North Yorkshire (pages 166–73). Wholescale restoration of medieval churches took place at the same time.

The change in emphasis from preaching to the celebration of the service of Holy Communion and the adoption of Gothic architecture had profound implications for the furnishings of both new and old churches as already mentioned. The importance of the chancel and its relationship to the congregation now became more important than the contact between the pulpit and the congregation. In new churches this could be arranged from the start. In older churches it meant that chancels were brought back into regular use, stone altars were reinstated with choir stalls to the sides. Three-decker pulpits were removed

Trust churches are rich in monuments of all periods, and reflect the religious and social attitudes of their time. Here, fourteenth-century knights at Allerton Mauleverer, West Yorkshire, lie in the pious medieval tradition of hands joined in prayer.

and replaced with smaller structures. So too were box pews; not only did they impede a view of the chancel, they represented a stratification of society that many clergy now found unacceptable in a place of Christian worship. They were replaced by the standard pine seating we see today. Stone flags were replaced throughout the church by colourful, highly glazed encaustic tiles. Funeral hatchments were removed to lessen the implied link between the Church and the aristocracy. All this swept away the feeling of contact with people of past generations. Church interiors now had an essentially modern, Victorian feeling.

Some smaller, remoter and poorer churches escaped this re-ordering. Their rectors might be more conservative, or their congregations could not afford the expense. Many of these churches have passed to the Trust. It is interesting to hear the exclamations of surprise and delight of visitors entering an interior where Jane Austen and her characters would be completely at home. The re-ordering of Georgian interiors has been criticised in the past but nostalgia should not be allowed

to obscure the fact that such churches can be unsuitable for the celebration of modern liturgies, although some parochial churches large and small still retain them. The box pews and the stone floors certainly cannot be popular with the people who clean them. The principal criticism of Victorian 'restorations' is that they did not restore – they attempted to 'improve', according to the aesthetic tastes of the time. Sections of buildings such as a chancel or an aisle or in many cases an entire church were all but demolished and rebuilt in a style of Gothic more agreeable to the restorers. Admittedly, many Victorian clergy inherited dilapidated buildings following widespread neglect in the eighteenth century and chose the easier option of demolition rather than repair. The policy of modern organisations in charge of ancient buildings is very different, as the description of the work of the Churches Conservation Trust in the Preface illustrates.

The special collective characteristics of most Trust churches have been identified as their memorably secret and beautiful locations, their splendid or simple architecture, their elegant or rustic furnishings and their atmospherically unrestored interiors. I have visited well over 1,000 churches in England, of which those belonging to the Trust account for only a few per cent, yet if I were to list twenty of the most memorable, taking all factors into account, there would be about ten Trust churches among them.

The Trust makes every effort to ensure that visits to its churches are enjoyable and rewarding. The experiences of the present writer, who has no formal connection with the Trust, and those of countless other visitors who have recorded their appreciation in visitors' books, are a confirmation that it has succeeded. Because of their remoteness, many Trust churches will not be discovered by chance and will need to be identified before travelling. The obvious starting points are the Trust's website and its county and regional leaflets, which give exact locations and directions, an outline of what is to be seen and details of access. The latter varies; some Trust churches are open all day, every day. In other cases they must be kept locked for security reasons, in which case the addresses of nearby keyholders will be displayed on the door or in the porch. (Here a word of thanks to those always friendly and obliging people living in cottages and farmhouses, who come to their front doors from kitchens, meal tables or gardens to hand over the key at all times of the day). A few churches are open at specified times on specified days. It is easier to gain entry than it is at many churches that are still actively parochial. The Trust has care of irreplaceable historic treasures inside its buildings, but far from locking them away to be seen only with permission and under supervision it positively encourages the public to visit. When a small church is rather inconspicuous in a town or country, a prominent easel board indicating CHURCH OPEN may be positioned on a grass verge or pavement outside. A street map, on a scale of about 3 inches to the mile, which indicates churches even when they are considerable distances off-road will be useful. A pair of stout shoes is also recommended in many cases. Inside the churches there is welcoming literature, including a well written informative guidebook. The churches are immaculately clean and well cared for. Fresh flowers on altars and window sills demonstrate the extent of the respect and affection of local people for a place that has served their parents, grandparents and perhaps many generations before that. Every need of visitors is catered for, such as electric lighting which may switch on automatically as they enter. Visitors are naturally invited to make a donation in a wallbox before leaving, but there are no entrance fees as there are at historic houses, and at most cathedrals also nowadays.

The emphasis in this Introduction and in this book as a whole may give the unintended impression that the author and the Trust regard its churches solely as repositories of historic

At Strensham, Worcestershire, Sir Francis Russell (d. 1704) appears to appeal to his wife, who points him to heaven.

architecture and art or museums of social history. On the contrary, the wall plaques displayed outside each building state that the church 'although no longer required for regular worship remains a consecrated building'. Many of the churches are used for occasional services on patronal feast days and at Easter and Christmas.

W.D. Caröe (1857–1938) was one of the most distinguished English architects practising in the decades around 1900, particularly noted for his sensitive restorations of ancient churches which respected their historical integrity in a way that many Victorian restorations had not. In his introduction to his book on the late medieval church at Sefton, Merseyside, where he had been a choirboy and which he had restored he wrote:

For indeed, the greatest glory of a building is not in its stones, nor in its gold. Its glory is in its age and in that deep sense of voicefulness which we feel in walls which have long been washed by the passing waves of humanity.

There are today few buildings in England where this 'voicefulness' of 'passing waves of humanity' can be more palpably experienced than in the churches now cared for by the Churches Conservation Trust. The organisation that has ensured this deserves every support from churchgoers and non-churchgoers alike who know that its churches have been part of England's history, are part of its present and must be part of its future.

A NOTE ON THE CHOICE OF CONTENTS AND THE ORDER OF PRESENTATION

A book that described all of the Trust's 340 churches in any meaningful way in photographs and text would have required several volumes. A selection of about a third of them could have been described briefly with a minimum of photographs but that seemed an unsatisfactory compromise. In this book, thirty-six of the churches have been chosen that are geographically and historically representative in terms of architecture and furnishings. Hopefully this has allowed sufficient space for a comprehensive portrait of each church that might provide the reader with the equivalent of a personal visit. Nonetheless this selectivity has meant that many outstandingly interesting churches have been omitted. I have not hesitated to spend some time in each case describing the church's surroundings as they are so much part of the experience. Of course nothing in a book can equate with the real thing and

perhaps some readers will be encouraged to visit the churches that are described – and the three hundred or more that are not.

It seemed desirable to have some discernible system in the order in which the chosen churches were described. Any kind of alphabetical would have little meaning and any kind of geographical order would have been difficult when travelling in all directions of the compass. Although the book is in no way intended to be a history of English architectural periods and styles it was possible to see that if the chapters were arranged in a broadly chronological sequence based on the ages of the churches it would give the reader some sense of the passage of time over the centuries if read consecutively. Only about half of the churches belong uniquely to one period built in a single campaign. The others are a complex mixture as a result of their evolution over many centuries and in these cases the most important and interesting features of architecture or furnishings have determined their position. Notwithstanding this, the chapters are self-contained and may be read in any order.

ACKNOWLEDGEMENTS

The text describes things I have seen myself. For details of architecture and art, for dates and for the history of people and events connected with the churches I have depended principally on two sources:

Firstly, the appropriate county volumes of Nikolaus Pevsner's monumental *Buildings of England* series. The first editions have now been extensively revised and enlarged by subsequent workers. Few people seriously interested in exploring ancient or modern English architecture travel without them. Unless otherwise stated, all direct quotations are from this source. (Penguin and Yale University Press, 1951–).

Secondly, the guide-booklets to individual churches published by the Trust, which can be purchased on site. Their scholarly descriptions of architectural history will satisfy experts in the field but their special value to the average visitor is their accounts of the local people and events involved in creating what is seen today. The text of this book would have been the poorer without them.

The poem on page 99 is reproduced by kind permission of the executors of Sir John Betjeman.

1. ST ANDREW, BYWELL, NORTHUMBERLAND

A REMINDER OF EARLY CHRISTIANITY IN SAXON ENGLAND

BYWELL IS ONLY TEN MILES WEST of the centre of Newcastle-upon-Tyne, yet light years away in its secret seclusion on the north bank of the River Tyne. The approach from the south is across wide open moorland covering a series of broad flat-topped hills on the eastern edge of the north Pennines. The road drops down sharply to the valley of the Tyne, where the land changes suddenly from the harsh to the lush. Bywell is signposted off a road between Blaydon (Newcastle) and Hexham that follows the river on the south side. An eighteenth-century bridge crosses to the north side into Bywell, a parish without any clearly defined village centre. All around, a wealth of large trees, many of them several hundred years old, form a canopy over the road. These, and the absence of cultivation, give the impression of ancient parkland rather than modern farmland. The impression is confirmed by glimpses of three great houses, one of which is a fifteenth-century castellated tower house, a large version of the pele towers that were used as defended homes in the dangerous Scottish border country of the Middle Ages. Bywell appears to visitors now as a little enclave of the landed aristocracy. Shortly, a cul-de-sac lane branches off the road to end a short distance from the river, where there are four buildings, although each is partly hidden from the others by trees and high hedges. There is eighteenth-century Bywell Hall, a seventeenth-century vicarage and the extraordinary sight of two churches facing each other across the lane. An isolated rural church is far from unusual in England but two within 50 yards of each other is a rarity. Each stands in its own large churchyard separated by a corner of the grounds of the Hall.

The rarity of this group of buildings is the greater because both churches have substantial Saxon parts: St Andrew's, which is cared for by the Trust, and St Peter's, which is the parish church. Although there are only about 500 churches in England that pre-date the Norman Conquest, the

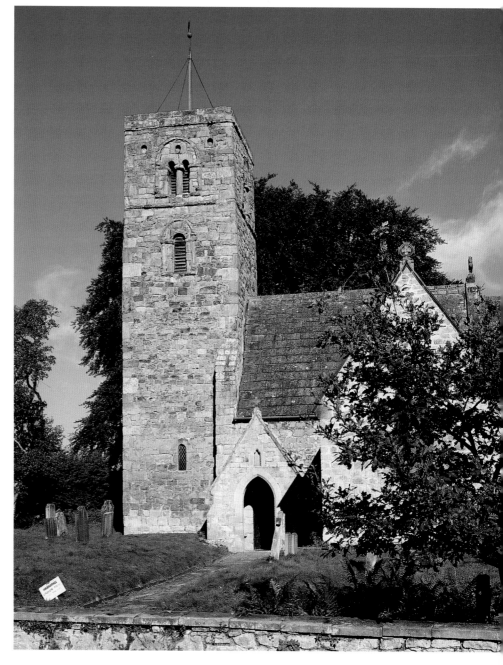

South view of St Andrew's, which is hidden away in a secret part of a wooded river valley. It has an excellent example of a complete tenth-century Saxon tower.

presence of two here together is not so remarkable given the history of the area. Northumbria was among the first of the Saxon heptarchy (or seven kingdoms) to be converted to Christianity when King Edwin (r. 616–33) married the daughter of King Ethelbert of Kent, who had been converted by St Augustine shortly after the latter had arrived in Kent in 597. Under Edwin's successor Oswald, Northumbria became dominant over the other kingdoms for some generations and a centre for the further conversion of England to Christianity. As well as having contact with Kent and Roman Christianity, Oswald was able to call on the monks at the monastery at Iona off the west coast of Scotland founded in the 560s by St Columba. The seventh century was a heroic age in Northumbrian Christianity, led by men of high intellect, total spiritual commitment and unstoppable energy. They included such bishops and abbots as St Aidan (d. 651), St Cedd (d. 664), St Cuthbert (634–87), St Benedict Biscop (628–89), St Wilfrid (633–707) and the Venerable Bede (673–737). They founded and worked from great monasteries such as Jarrow, Monkwearmouth, Hexham, Lindisfarne and York, from where their influence stretched from England across the North Sea to mainland Europe. After the Saxon period, the continued use and extensions of the two Bywell churches in the Middle Ages may be connected to the fact that the boundary between two adjacent baronies, Baliol and Bolbec ran through the parish.

St Andrew's is a medium-sized building with chancel, north and south transepts, nave and west tower. It is built of local brown sandstone. The Saxon features of the tower are easily recognised.

RIGHT *The megaliths forming the corner stones of the tower are set 'side alternate' – a typical form of Saxon masonry, possibly in imitation of contemporary timber-framed buildings.*

FAR RIGHT *More characteristic features of Saxon architecture are seen in the upper parts of the tower. The top belfry stage has narrow, twin round-arched openings separated by a baluster set in mid-wall. Below is a wider window with pilaster mouldings to the sides. The circular openings are also original.*

It is tall and, unlike medieval towers, is unbuttressed and has no set-offs. The corners are made up of stones much larger than the rest, of square cross-section and laid 'side alternate', a form of masonry related to the archtypal Saxon feature known as 'long and short work'. It may derive from the masons' attempt to imitate the corners of contemporary timber-framed structures. Above the roofline of the nave there is a window contained within a blank arch with pilaster-like supports. Above this there is a characteristically Saxon belfy stage, with double openings separated by a baluster set in the middle of the wall and again surrounded by a superarch. 'All this work is a sign of a dim consciousness of the Romanesque style on the continent.' The arch-heads of the openings in the tower are each carved out of a single stone because Saxon masons had difficulty in building wider arches made up of several stones as in later periods. It is difficult to date the tower since only a handful of Saxon churches have any contemporary documentation. On stylistic grounds scholars have placed it in the late Saxon period 950–1000, well after the heroic period of the great saints mentioned above. However, it has been suggested that the Bywell tower may be

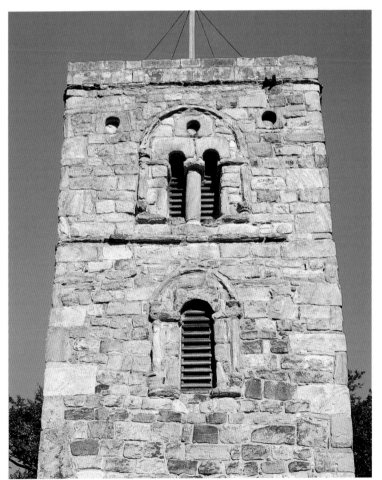

a heightening of a porch of a much older church as known at Hexham and Corbridge near by. The west end of the nave adjacent to the tower is probably Saxon, but everything to the east of that was extended in the thirteenth century or later. There are echoes of the church's early origins in the remains of the shaft of a Saxon cross in the chancel.

The church underwent a major restoration in the nineteenth century, when clearly no expense was spared. The big heavy south door has arabesque ironwork in a convincing thirteenth-century style. In the chancel the altar has a striking mosaic reredos brilliant with gold and other colours depicting saints, which include St Andrew, the church's patron. The mosaic is continued in the chancel floor, making a change from the usual encaustic tiles of the period. The stained glass is also of a higher standard than much nineteenth-century work. It was during this restoration that twenty-five medieval gravestones with incised decoration were set into the external and internal walls. Most of them date from 1150–1250 and some have emblems showing the occupations of the deceased such as swords for knights.

Visitors to St Andrew's should cross the lane to St Peter's, a much larger church which is generally open and welcoming, with its own interesting Saxon, medieval and post-medieval features. The churchyard slopes down to the banks of the River Tyne as it flows through Bywell to Newcastle. Before leaving, this is a good spot to reflect on the remarkable combination of natural scenery and man-made history in this memorable place.

A diocese cannot support two churches adjacent to each other like this today and St Andrew's was declared redundant in 1973 and handed over to the Churches Conservation Trust in 1975.

2. ST ANDREW, WINTERBORNE TOMSON, DORSET

A NORMAN PLAN RELATED TO THE EARLIEST CHRISTIAN CHURCHES

NAMES OF VILLAGES OFTEN OCCUR in linked groups connected by some geographical feature, and understanding their origins can add an extra interest to exploring the English landscape. There are ten or more Winterborne (or Winterbourne) villages in Dorset and several others elsewhere in southern England. This is an area of chalk, a very porous rock which occurs at or just below the surface and allows surface water to penetrate rapidly. As a result in seasons of low rainfall streams and small rivers quickly disappear underground. Only in winter is there sufficient rain to create an overground stream. The Old English (Saxon) for stream is *bourne* (the modern Scottish 'burn') and hence the words winterbourne or winterborne. Villages lying on a particular winterborne then have to be designated by a second title. Thus the hamlet of Winterborne Tomson flows through the land that belonged to a Saxon man who was the son of Thomas. It is about 8 miles south-west of Blandford Forum (not a Roman town despite its name) in the centre of one of the most unspoilt rural counties in England. Winterborne Tomson

This smallest of Norman churches has a semi-circular (apsidal) east end, which derives from the first churches of fourth-century Rome. The building is constructed of local flint and limestone.

The complete set of early-eighteenth-century box pews with a charming plastered wagon roof above.

is so small that it is not marked on most road atlases, consisting of only a manor house and a few cottages grouped around a tiny church at the end of a private road.

The church has an aisleless nave with a semi-circular chancel at the east end and a weatherboarded bell-turret at the west end. Like many buildings in Dorset, it is constructed of flint, which always occurs with chalk, with limestone dressings. At first sight there may seem little externally to indicate the date except for the large windows with square hood moulds, which are late-sixteenth or early-seventeenth century.

The clue to further dating lies in the semi-circular east end, which is unusual: the great majority of English churches are square-ended. However, a rounded chancel is a very ancient feature of Christian architecture dating back to the fourth century in Rome, soon after the Emperor Constantine first legalised Christianity and then made it the official religion of the Roman empire. Christians, now free to worship in public adopted the plan of the Roman basilicas for their first churches, rather than the much more impressive temples with their inherently pagan associations. Basilicas were relatively humble buildings used for administrative purposes consisting of an aisled hall with a semi-circular extension at one end known as an apse, which was occupied by a presiding senator, magistrate or other official. Often enlarged and elaborated, this apse was to become the chancel of Christian cathedrals and churches where a priest now presided. Some Saxon and many Norman cathedrals and churches imported this feature from western mainland Europe where it was widespread in the Romanesque style of architecture between the tenth and twelfth centuries. The English, as they emerged with their own identity as a nation in the thirteenth century, seemed to have disliked these semi-circular apses. In new churches chancels were built with square ends and often the apses of existing churches were rebuilt in squared-off form. There was evidently no inclination to do this at Winterborne Tomson, so we have here a tiny, remote English church of the mid-twelfth century which relates directly back to Imperial Rome and early Christianity. The shallow buttresses around the apse are Norman too, as is a small original window in the nave.

Despite its size and lack of distinguished architecture Nikolaus Pevsner writes quite lyrically about the church — quite unusual for a rather severe architectural historian who must have seen and described over fifteen thousand churches in the county volumes of his *Buildings Of England*. He calls it 'a gem of a village church, sufficiently different from others to arrest attention at once and an interior which fulfills all one's expectations'. It is no surprise that this interior preserves a complete set of early-eighteenth-century furnishings. Victorian rectors would have had little to get their teeth into in such a confined space. Box pews fill the nave on either side of a centre aisle and there is a two-decker pulpit. There would not have been room for a three-decker in such a low building. The apse is separated from the nave by a simple open screen. Pevsner was impressed by the

'charming' plastered wagon roof, whose ribs extend into the apse where they are set radially to fit the plan. There is a west gallery, probably for singers and instrumentalists who provided the music before the widespread use of organs. The interior is beautifully unified, since the work was obviously done in one campaign, the benefactor being no less than William Wake, archbishop of Canterbury from 1716 to 1737.

The church was much loved by Thomas Hardy, author of the rather dark novels set in rural Dorset in places such as this. It fell into disrepair in the late nineteenth century. In Hardy's memory the architect A.R. Powys restored the church in 1931 under the auspices of the Society for the Protection of Ancient Buildings, which was founded by William Morris in 1877 and was in some ways a forerunner of the Churches Conservation Trust. It was an 'unassuming and sensitive' restoration of the type that the Trust now adopts in all of its own work. Powys' restoration is recorded on a beautifully inscribed slate tablet in the nave.

The church was invested in the Trust in 1974.

In memory of Albert Reginald Powys 1881-1936 C.B.E. Architect & Writer, the devoted servant for over 25 years of the Society for the Protection of Ancient Buildings, who is buried in this churchyard as he desired. This church, greatly loved by Thomas Hardy, was saved from ruin by the sale of certain of his mss which paid for work done here 1929-31. As they shared Life Love & Death this stone is set by Faith, wife of A.R. Powys

A beautifully cut inscription records the restoration of the then derelict church in 1931 by a local architect in memory of the novelist Thomas Hardy, who loved this place.

3. ST MARGARET, HALES AND ST GREGORY, HECKINGHAM, NORFOLK

TWO SISTER CHURCHES IN NEIGHBOURING PARISHES

THE TWO VILLAGES ARE A MILE APART, about 10 miles south-east of Norwich. They are close enough to main roads to be easily accessible, far enough away to have rural peace. Pevsner wrote: 'Hales is a perfect Norman village church, the sister of Heckingham.' They are similar in so many ways that there can be no doubt that they were built by the same team of masons. Both are small, and both have an aisleless nave and a lower chancel with a semi-circular, or apsidal, east end. These apses are the type seen at Winterborne Tomson, Dorset, deriving from the pre-Christian basilicas of ancient Rome whose plan was adopted in the earliest Christian churches in the city in the fourth century (pages 29–31).

The most striking feature at Hales is the western round tower. The part of the Heckingham tower visible in the photograph is octagonal but it is circular at ground level. The change to the upper part was made in the later Middle Ages. Although round towers are a rarity in most of England, they are relatively common throughout East Anglia. The late H. Munro Cautley, who was an expert in all things ecclesiastical in medieval East Anglia counted 119 in Norfolk, 41 in Suffolk and 8 in Essex. There are a few in Lincolnshire and elsewhere. One theory to explain the number of round towers in this region suggests that it is an example of design adapting to the availability of materials. East Anglia is an area of flint, which always occurs in chalk country such as this. Flint was used widely in churches large and small, grand and humble. Unlike other stones it is not quarried from underground beds and cut for use. Flint occurs in totally irregular small pieces at or near the surface over wide areas. The pieces can be cleaved and the outer surfaces squared-off but it cannot be cut into blocks. It is suitable for building in that it is very hard and weather resistant. When

ABOVE *Hales Church (above) and Heckingham church (below) have similar ground plans with semi-circular east ends. Both were built with round towers but the one at Heckingham was made octagonal in the Middle Ages.*

RIGHT *The round tower at Hales and those elsewhere in East Anglia are all built of flint. Such circular structures lend themselves to the use of small irregularly shaped pieces of flint, which cannot be cut into square blocks.*

it is used with plenty of mortar it can be used in straight walling but not to create corners, which need blocks of cut stone. The theory relating to the round towers in small East Anglian churches is that this shape eliminated the need for limestone to be brought in from counties further west to create the corners of a square tower. The history of flint round towers dates from the late Saxon period. Cautley considers that about forty of the Norfolk towers pre-date the Conquest as shown by their typically Saxon openings (Bywell, pages 26–8).

All the features at Hales and Heckingham are late Norman. The eastern apses have the shallow pilaster-like buttresses of the time and the windows are round-headed although in the Middle Ages some of the latter were replaced with Gothic whose pointed arches break up the regular rhythm of the round arches. The main doorways of the two churches show without doubt that the same team of masons was at work at both. They are strikingly similar tours-de-force of Norman carving and design, showing all the technical skill and artistic virility and imagination of the best craftsmen. The capitals of the columns which support the arches have similar decoration. The arches themselves have the ubiquitous Norman zig-zag, and in addition there is unusual bobbin-like decoration, rosettes and wheels, all of it crisply carved and very well preserved.

Both churches have thatched roofs, which provide a homely touch not as uncommon in East Anglia as elsewhere.

The interiors of both churches have a number of interesting features, including Norman fonts and medieval wall paintings and screens. It is, however, for the towers and the stone carving that one remembers these two twin sisters.

Following the amalgamation of the two parishes in 1973 Hales church was handed over to the Trust in 1974. Further amalgamations resulted in Heckingham following in 1993.

ABOVE *The doorway at Hales. It is a tour de force of Norman carving, imaginative in design and forcefully virile in execution.*

BELOW *The same masons were clearly at work in creating the various decorative elements of the doorway arches, zig-zag, bobbins, rosettes and wheels at Hales (left) and at Heckingham (right).*

4. ST MICHAEL, UPTON CRESSETT, SHROPSHIRE

NORMAN POWER ON A SMALL SCALE

THE PARISH OF UPTON CRESSETT (there is no village now as such) lies halfway between Bridgnorth and Much Wenlock on the eastern edge of the spectacular hill country of south Shropshire which includes the Long Myndd and Wenlock Edge. The roads keep mainly to the valleys – everything above that is a walker's paradise. A single-track lane that leaves the Bridgnorth to Much Wenlock road soon sinks below the level of the fields on either side and the hedges rise higher still in a way reminiscent of deepest Devon. Motorists can hope that that they will not meet a tractor pulling a farmcart, a meeting that would severely test reverse driving skills on the frequent blind bends. After passing a few isolated farmhouses and cottages, the lane comes to a dead end after 2 miles alongside two remarkable buildings, St Michael's church and Upton Hall. Even on such a confined road as this it is easy to miss the church, which is small and set well back in a large churchyard. A few yards further on, Upton Hall and its impressive detached gatehouse next to the road will never be missed. They are both excellent examples of Tudor brickwork: the Hall of *c.*1540 and the gatehouse of

The essentially Norman structure of the church is hidden by later medieval additions and Victorian windows.

The late medieval timber porch has massive rafters, tie-beams and braces.

The original Norman church had an aisleless nave and a straight-ended chancel. Such two-cell structures are typical of the humbler Norman village churches. In the thirteenth century the chancel was provided with a south chapel as big as the chancel itself. At the same time, a north aisle was added but this was demolished in the eighteenth century. The little weather-boarded belfry with a squat lead-covered tower is also a later addition. The late medieval porch has a sturdy timber roof with massive rafters, tie-beams and braces. In a Victorian restoration a number of the original windows were replaced.

When seen from the churchyard the later work obscures the essential Norman character of the church but the Norman origins are evident in the doorway within the porch. The supporting shafts of the round-headed arches have capitals with thinly incised decoration, clearly done by masons much less skilful and ambitious than those at Hales and Heckingham (pages 32–4).

Inside, the tiny nave is almost as wide as long. It has something of the earthy, claustrophobic atmosphere of a contemporary castle chamber, only dimly lit by two slit-like original windows on the south side. The effect is slightly relieved by the whitewashed walls and the later clay tiles. The memorable feature is the chancel arch, which spans almost the entire width of the nave and dominates the confined space. The three orders of shafts and the arches decorated with zig-zag make it an effective statement of Norman power and artistic virility. The tub-shaped font is decorated with a circle of incised arches with cable moulding above and below.

In 1968, the remains of a medieval wall painting were discovered in the early-thirteenth-century chancel chapel, probably made when the chapel was built. An angel with wings and parts of other figures can be made out surrounded by foliage trails. It may have been painted by the same hand that did the extensive and much better preserved paintings at Claverley some 10 miles to the east.

After the Second World War the Hall was unoccupied for a time and the scattered population of the parish declined. The church was closed in 1959 on safety grounds and declared redundant in 1970, by which time it was semi-derelict. It was passed to the Trust in 1972, which carried out an extensive but sensitive restoration which left its ancient character intact.

c.1580. The Hall is a rebuilding of much earlier manor houses that have occupied the site since the Norman Conquest. The estates passed through various families until the fourteenth century when an heiress married into the French Cressett family which has given its name to the place ever since. The grounds of the Hall let onto the churchyard without division. Such proximity was commonplace throughout the Middle Ages when all lived as part of a feudal family. Although Upton Cressett is now a parish without a village the network of bumps and hollows in a field near the church indicates the site of a former medieval settlement. Late-fourteenth-century documents show that the decline of the village was well advanced even at that time, perhaps connected with outbreaks of the Black Death. When the occupants of the Hall enclosed 40 acres of arable land in the sixteenth century to create a park, the village disappeared completely.

ABOVE *The diminutive nave is dominated by the chancel arch, which spans almost its entire width, exuding all the raw forcefulness of Norman architecture.*

RIGHT *The norman tub-font is decorated overall with blank arches and cable mouldings above and below.*

FAR RIGHT *The fragmentary wall painting of c.1200 shows an angel surrounded by foliage trails.*

5. ST PETER, NORTHAMPTON

SHOW CHURCH FOR A GREAT NORMAN CASTLE

NORTHAMPTON WAS AN IMPORTANT TOWN in the Saxon kingdom of Mercia under King Offa in the eighth century and later under the Wessex kings. Immediately adjacent to the church of St Peter in the town centre, a series of Anglo Saxon buildings were excavated in 1980–2. They were interpreted as a royal palace or residence, and at least one, possibly several churches. The Normans built a castle here a few years after the Conquest, which became one of the largest and most powerful is England where royal councils and parliaments were held. Its situation on a mound protected by the River Nene on two sides was ideal. Almost nothing remains of the castle, which was demolished in the nineteenth century to make way for the main line railway and station. A postern gate in a wall and several display boards erected by the city council around the site are the only visual reminders.

St Peter's church was built just beyond the outer bailey in c.1150 and was not therefore strictly a garrison church. Its association with the castle, however, may be taken for granted. Its size and grandeur show that it was built at considerable expense for grand state occasions involving nobility and royal visits. It was certainly not built for ordinary parochial purposes, since there were already two parishes only a few hundred yards away: the famous round church of the Holy Sepulchre built in c.1110 and All Saints near the Market Square, both of which are still in existence. Successive generations of the de Senslis family, Earls of Northampton, were responsible for building the castle and these churches. There were, in addition,

The south view shows the long unbroken line of nave and chancel, built in c.1150. The grassy foreground and trees belie the situation close to a busy town centre.

ABOVE LEFT *The Norman west tower was altered during repairs in c.1600. The infilled doorway has an arch carved with saltire crosses. Note the unusual banding of brown sandstone and grey limestone.*

ABOVE RIGHT *The east end was rebuilt entirely by George Gilbert Scott in 1850 in a style said to follow the original.*

LEFT *The broad arch between nave and tower is a sumptuously ornate example of Norman carving.*

LEFT *Tower arch detail showing the inventive variety of motifs: trellis work on the shafts, scallops on the capitals and zig-zags and lozenges on the arches.*

ABOVE *Four examples of the fourteen capitals in the nave arcade, all of which are different. None has religious symbolism. Clockwise from top left: two dog-like animals with enormous tails and tongues; grotesque faces with bulging eyes; complex interlace patterns; capital and arch with zig-zag above showing the same banding of stonework seen outside.*

a number of early Norman priory churches. Northampton town centre is therefore a good example of the powerful partnership between State and Church that the Normans originally established in Normandy and then in cities and towns of conquered lands.

St Peter's and its small churchyard in Marefair are now surrounded by typically modern hotels, offices and flats. Architectural photographers are fortunate in that the land to the south is open grassland falling away from the church, providing an excellent view of the whole building in early spring, before the surrounding trees come into leaf and obscure the view. The plan and elevation are unusual as there is no break in height or width between the nave and

chancel. Apart from the low west tower the building runs as one from west to east, a continuity emphasised by the long unbroken line of clerestory windows and the blank arcading between them.

At the west end the tower had become ruinous by 1600 and was rebuilt. The position was shifted one bay to the east, cutting into the nave. The stonework is striking. Northampton lies on the geological boundary between the dark brown calcareous sandstone of the central midlands and the silver-grey limestone of the east midlands. The two stones are used in alternate banding in the lower part of the tower and more irregularly higher up. During the rebuilding the former Norman entrance in the west wall of the tower was filled in and given a window. Its arch was modified to appear as a broad flat band with carvings of saltire crosses, knots and other motifs. The corners of the tower have unusual semi-circular buttresses. At the other end of the building the chancel was completely rebuilt by George Gilbert Scott in 1850. The east wall has three stages of round-headed windows and a central circular buttress. It is stated that Scott followed the original Norman work, although that would have been rare in a Victorian restoration when architects were more inclined to 'improve' upon the original according to their own views.

The 'outstandingly ornate' interior is one of the most impressive and exciting Norman parish churches in England. As the exterior revealed, it runs continuously from east to west without even the division provided by a chancel arch. The arcades between nave and aisles have alternating supports of round and quatrefoil cross-section, a feature normally only seen in cathedrals and abbey churches. All the piers have finely carved capitals which combine the masculine virility of

LEFT *A late Saxon or early Norman gravestone now set erect. A trail of vine stems and leaves is inhabited by the face of a Green Man and by birds and animals.*

RIGHT *Monument to William Smith (1769–1839), one of the founders of the modern science of geology.*

early Norman work with a little of the delicacy of the later period. There are fourteen capitals in all, each with four faces and no two of these are alike. None of the carvings has any Christian symbolism, which is not unusual in Norman work. There are mythical animals, grotesques and many complex interlaced designs. The banding of brown sandstone and grey limestone seen outside is continued in the arcade arches decorated with zig-zag. The arch between nave and tower is the most spectacular larger piece of sculpture. It is a massive structure with three orders of shafts which like the arches above them are decorated overall in a variety of motifs This tower arch is something of a puzzle. It would be usual to see an arch of this size and opulence separating nave and chancel where it would be seen by the whole congregation during services. It appears that the original patron, Earl de Senslis did not want clergy and high status laity in this church separated at services.

The gravestone now set vertically at the east end of the south aisle is yet another interesting piece of carving. It consists of entwined vine stems and foliage 'inhabited' by animals, birds and a Green Man, the ubiquitous medieval fertility symbol with leaves emanating from his mouth. It has been variously dated as late Saxon or early Norman. Certainly, such inhabited vine trails were used in many Anglo Saxon cross shafts. The stone has been associated with the shrine of St Ragener, a Saxon killed by the Danes in 870. It is known that Edward the Confessor erected a magnificent shrine to the saint in the church. There is only one significant monument of more recent times, that to William Smith (1769–1839), whose conclusions based on his observations of stratification of rocks and fossils formed the basis of the modern science of geology, a science which in the later nineteenth century was to overturn the biblical dating of the creation of the world and cause much controversy.

The photographs were taken on a quiet day at a quiet time of the year when there were no other visitors. It was a remarkable experience working here

TO HONOUR THE NAME OF
WILLIAM SMITH, LL.D.
THIS MONUMENT IS ERECTED BY HIS FRIENDS AND FELLOW LABOURERS IN THE FIELD OF BRITISH GEOLOGY.
BORN 23RD MARCH 1769 AT CHURCHILL IN OXFORDSHIRE AND TRAINED TO THE PROFESSION OF A CIVIL ENGINEER AND

alone for several hours absorbed with the camera but mentally visualising and hearing the place full of Norman nobles and their retainers from the castle at mass on Sundays and saints' days. How religious would have been the atmosphere among these rough military men? Many more peaceable generations followed of course until the last regular service was held here on Easter Sunday in 1988 after which the church was handed over to the Trust.

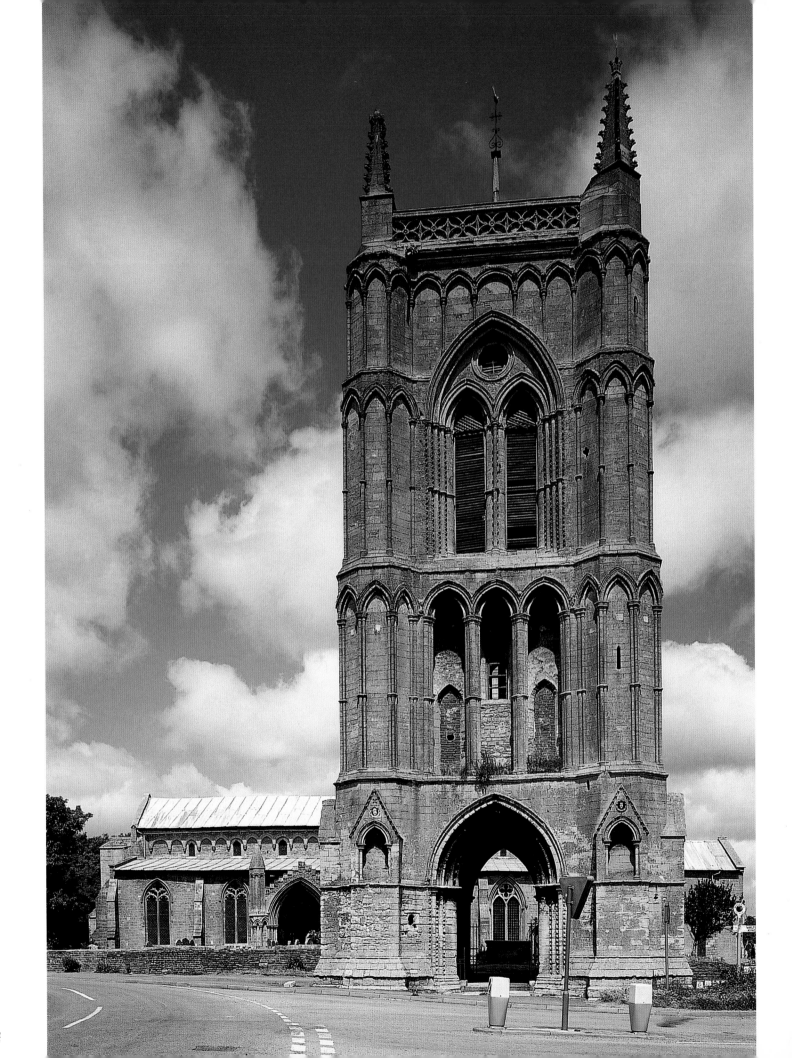

6. ST MARY (THE TOWER), WEST WALTON, NORFOLK

A SUMPTUOUS FLOWERING OF EARLY ENGLISH GOTHIC ARCHITECTURE

THE SMALL VILLAGE OF WEST WALTON is a few miles south-west of Kings Lynn in the fenlands of north-west Norfolk, adjacent to the Lincolnshire Fens. To the visitor the region can have an empty, melancholic atmosphere. The large dykes that criss-cross the flat landscape and the smaller ditches that border most of the fields show that immense effort has been necessary to keep the land drained and workable over the centuries. The Norfolk Fens have an extraordinary number of fine churches, probably more per square mile than any other place in England, although the reason is not clear. The churches span the centuries from twelfth-century Norman to late medieval (such as the nearby Wiggenhall villages, pages 76–9) and so they cannot be ascribed to the prosperity of any particular time, like the 'Wool Churches' of the Cotswolds.

The village houses are grouped around the junction of several minor roads about a mile from the Kings Lynn–Wisbech road. It is not an especially picturesque village by the standards of others in Norfolk. However, the characteristically East Anglian picture sign at the entrance to the village shows that the villagers are proud of having one piece of architecture of national importance in their midst – the great detached bell tower of their parish church. The church of St Mary is an outstanding example of the first period of Gothic architecture in England from c.1180–1250 known as Early English. The Romanesque (Norman) churches described previously, particularly the larger ones like Northampton (pages 38–43) relied on massively thick walls and internal piers to support the superstructure, so creating an effect of overwhelming heaviness and power. The creation of the Gothic style in Northern France in the early twelfth century brought together a number of constructional techniques, such as the pointed arch and flying buttresses, which enabled the weight of even a large building to be transmitted to the ground at certain points only along its length, removing the necessity for continuous thick walls and piers within.

OPPOSITE *The detached bell tower at the entrance to the churchyard is a rarity in England. Proudly tall and broad, it displays many of the structural and decorative features of Early English Gothic.*

ABOVE *The tower seen from the west end of the church. The archways below act as entrances to the churchyard.*

LEFT *The village sign is typically East Anglian. The people clearly identify themselves with the great mid-thirteenth-century tower of their parish church. Sheep were the basis of much of the prosperity of medieval Norfolk.*

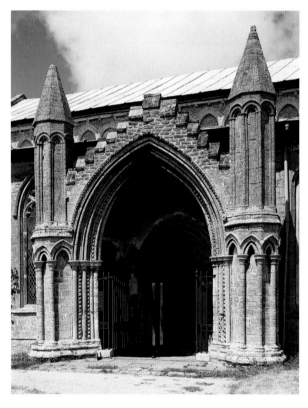

LEFT *When seen from inside the churchyard, the lack of an attached tower gives the church a rather barn-like appearance.*

LEFT BELOW *The two doorways have a sumptuousness unprarlleled in parish churches. Left: The south porch and doorway are everywhere embellished with panelling and deeply undercut mouldings. Right: The west doorway has two twin doors separated by a central column, a feature normally seen only in cathedrals and abbey churches.*

RIGHT *The splendid nave arcade. The piers have detached subsidiary shafts of dark Purbeck marble and stiff-leaf capitals.*

Without the need for continuous stone walling, much greater areas could be opened up for glass. So lightness as opposed to heaviness and light as opposed to dark were the hallmarks of the new style. Moreover, steeply pointed arches as opposed to round arches produce a new aesthetic, one of upwardly aspiring movement as opposed to the more earthbound Romanesque. Gothic came to England in a fully developed way in the rebuilding of Canterbury Cathedral in the 1180s.

In its simplest expression, the Early English style can be calm, cool and rather unexciting.

Arches outside and inside have simple chamfers and piers are round or octagonal with insignificant capitals. When the necessary money was available, the imagination and skill of the best masons could transform this into something exuberantly ornate. The money and skill were available at such Early English cathedrals as Salisbury, Wells and elsewhere. They were also clearly available at West Walton, where the church and the tower have all the external structural and decorative features of Early English at its most sumptuous.

The church was built in the 1240s, towards

TOP *Nave pier detail. The stiff-leaf foliage is a leitmotif of Early English. The leaves here appear to be blowing in the wind, cut by a master carver.*

ABOVE *The deeply undercut roll mouldings on shafts and arches at the junction of nave and chancel produce the rippling effect beloved of Gothic masons.*

the end of the Early English period. The rare feature of a detached bell tower was built a few years after the body of the church was complete, although it was undoubtedly conceived from the start. It stands about 30 yards south of the church at the entrance to the churchyard. Detached bell towers derive from the Italian *campanili* of the eleventh and twelfth centuries in a country where they were popular. There are only about fifty in England, many of them along the Welsh border where they had a defensive character (such as at Richards Castle, pages 137–40). The tower and and the church behind it are built of silver-grey Jurassic limestone from Barnack near Peterborough, which was a source of good building stone throughout the Middle Ages for East Anglia, which has little good stone of its own. Barnack stone is hard enough to withstand the weather but soft enough for the elaborate carving that was required here. The tower is an impressive, powerful structure of three stages, broad as well as tall. The ground stage has open arches on all four sides acting as entrances into the churchyard as though it was a gatehouse as well as a belfry. The arches have gabled niches to left and right. In the stage above there are three tall narrow lancets with subsidiary side-shafts. Windows or unglazed openings like this are very characteristic of Early English and are an easy way to recognise the style. The bell-stage has lancets too, but here they are twinned under a super-arch. The massive polygonal buttresses which conceal the corners of the tower have more blank arcading of the lancet type. The decorated parapet and four corner pinnacles were added in the fifteenth century. The whole composition is a masterpiece of proportion and design. The reason for building a detached bell tower at West Walton is probably technical rather than defensive or aesthetic. The marshy subsoil of the fens provides a poor foundation for such a heavy structure as this. Had an attached tower collapsed it might have brought much of the church to the ground with it. A similar thing was done at Terrington St Clement near by although there the tower is only a few yards from the church.

The tower but not the church was vested in the Trust in 1987 but it would be inappropriate to leave without a brief visit to one of the finest parish churches in England. Lacking an attached tower the church behind inevitably has a rather barn-like appearance. The chancel is almost as long as the nave, as though there was a resident college of priests who would require the space for the daily offices. None of the windows in the nave or chancel is original, reflecting the desire of the Decorated and Perpendicular periods to have ever more light. The church has two very ornate original doorways. The main south door for everyday use has a deep stone porch. The steeply pointed front arch has multiple roll moldings. To the left and light are clasping polygonal buttresses with blank arcading of the type seen in the tower. The brickwork above is Tudor. The second entrance at the west end would have been used for special occasions such as the Easter ceremonies. It has two doorways with twin arches separated by a central column known as a trumeau. The whole is

The side walls of the chancel have the same blank arcading seen elsewhere on tower and church.

set within a round outer arch. The type is normally seen only in cathedrals and abbey churches.

The two doorways are a suitable introduction to the equally spectacular interior, which is distinguished principally by the magnificent arcade between nave and aisles. The arches rise from circular piers each surrounded by a ring of completely detached shafts of dark Purbeck marble. This shelly limestone (it is not a true marble in the geological sense) from the Dorset coast near Swanage was a very popular decorative stone in the thirteenth century in cathedrals and abbeys all over England who could afford the transport costs and its use here emphasises the wealth available at West Walton. The piers and the shafts have 'stiff-leaf' decoration, which is a form of three-leafed foliage based on the acanthus leaf. In the first years of Early English it was cut in low relief. Here in the later years of the period it was deeply undercut and became alive with movement as though blowing in a breeze from the open south and west doors. The arches

above have again deeply undercut roll moldings which produce a rippling effect beloved of the more skilled Gothic masons. It can be seen to even greater effect at the east end of the nave where it meets the chancel. Within the latter, the walls have the same blank arcading as in the tower, south porch and elsewhere. It was the Gothic aim to leave as little blank wall as possible.

The church is now much larger than needed for present day congregations and a few rows of chairs at the front of the nave are sufficient. The remainder of the nave consequently has the sense of spaciousness that it would have had originally. The floor of large irregular slabs of stone contributes to the atmosphere. All this indicates another church that escaped Victorian restoration when encaustic tiles would have been inserted beneath pine benches. This was the favourite church of John Piper (1902–93), landscape and architectural painter, stained glass artist and travelling companion of John Betjeman. It is easy to understand why.

7. ST ANTHONY, ST ANTHONY-IN-ROSELAND, CORNWALL

THE WATERSIDE HOME OF MONKS AND ADMIRALS

To THE EAST OF FALMOUTH on the opposite side of the inlet known as the Carrick Roads, Roseland is one of the remotest and most secretive of the peninsulas on the south Cornish coast. March or April is a good out-of-season time to visit. The holiday makers have not yet arrived and Roseland and similar places are quietly dreaming of their Celtic saints whose memory is perpetuated in so many of the county's place names. The Atlantic air is mild and the ground is alive with flowering shrubs and bulbs which have yet to appear in other parts of England. The peninsula reaches out to sea for about 6 miles, getting ever narrower as it approaches its two forked headlands. After the first few miles the road to the headland gets narrower too and burrows ever deeper below the surrounding fields and high hedges. For the last part of the journey travellers must be content with the speeds of former times.

Like many of the places described in this volume, St Anthony-in-Roseland, right at the end of the peninsula, is a parish without a village as such. The road drops down sharply to end abruptly on a little quayside on a small creek, a side-arm of a larger creek which stretches several miles inland from St Mawes Head. A quay generally pre-supposes a small community near by with business on the water. The surprise here is that the only community seems to be one apparently affluent family. An extensive lawn runs up from the quay to the long towered frontage of a nineteenth-century neo-Gothic mansion. The small spire of a church peeps above the roofline of the house. Apart from a few estate cottages hidden away in trees there are no other buildings.

The church is reached by returning a few hundred yards back up the road, crossing a stile and following a footpath beneath: a canopy of tall trees. At the time of my visit in late March a splash of red was provided by camellia bushes in full bloom just at the point where the church comes into view. Visitors are now at the back of the big house which is seen to be actually attached to the church. The churchyard looks out across blue water to the town of St Mawes on the opposite side of the creek. There are very

LEFT *Near the end of the Roseland Peninsula, the lawns of The Place, the home of the Spry family since the seventeenth century, run down to a quay on a small creek. From behind the house, the spire of the early medieval priory church of St Anthony peeps out above the roofline.*

RIGHT *The view from the churchyard across to the town of St Mawes.*

The way to the church is a woodland path brightened in March with camellias and daffodils. The rear of The Place, right, is attached to the church.

See Also — Alex Woodcock "Bestheads" Binder

few churches in England that have surroundings as unusual and beautiful as this. Christianity flourished in tenth century Cornwall in the Saxon diocese of Crediton and it is almost certain that there was a church on this site by that time. After the Norman Conquest the parish was given to the Augustinian Priory at Plympton, Devon, which established a 'cell' or subsidiary dependent house here with two monks known as canons. The members of the order were more involved in parochial work than the Benedictines and they manned St Anthony's as a parish church as much as a priory. The church is essentially Early English Gothic of the early thirteenth century. It consists of an aisleless nave, chancel and north and south transepts which were never subsequently

ABOVE *The south doorway is late Norman work carved in Caen Limestone from France. It was brought from Plympton Priory in Devon after rebuilding work there made it redundant. Its reuse here is an early example of recycling.*

BELOW *A corbel on one of the crossing piers shows a grinning man with horns and stiff-leaf decorations above.*

extended. The tiny population and the few canons in residence would never have required a larger building. The impressive south doorway is something of a puzzle. It is clearly of an earlier period to the rest of the church and the white stonework is very different from the sombre granite and iron-stained slate stones used elsewhere. It is an elaborate piece of Norman work with three orders of arches. The outer one is decorated with zig-zag, the middle one has continuous cusping while the inner one is plain. At the time that St Anthony's church was being built the Norman church at Plympton Priory was being extended. This must have produced some surplus fine quality masonry and the doorway of their church was probably sent to Roseland by sea, an early example of sensible recycling even if the result is a little incongruous. As at many major Norman establishments, the canons at Plympton had used Caen stone shipped over from France, which is the white limestone that now gleams so brilliantly in Cornish sunshine.

Inside the church the most impressive part is the area underneath the crossing. The four arches to nave, chancel and two transepts are good Early English work, financed as they were by a wealthy organisation. One of the capitals has a grinning horned head of a man. A doorway in the north aisle which formerly led into the canons' cloister and domestic quarters beyond now connects with the house.

The priory came to an end in 1538 when Henry VIII dissolved the monasteries. The nave and transepts of the church escaped destruction because they were parochial but the chancel used by the canons was demolished. The domestic buildings were also demolished and shortly afterwards became the first version of the house we see today, known from an early stage as 'The Place'. Ownership passed through a number of families until the house was purchased in 1649 by the Spry family who subsequently became extremely wealthy through marriage and business ventures. Fittingly for people living in such close proximity to the sea two successive heads of the family became admirals.

The Spry monuments form an interesting feature of the church. After a number of rather florid seventeenth century works, there are the impressive monuments to the two admirals. Richard Westmacott the Younger sculpted the white marble memorial to Sir Richard Spry, Admiral of the White who died in 1775. In the foreground the seated figure of Britannia leans on an urn with the arms of the the Sprys. Behind her, a view

The white marble monument to Sir Richard Spry, Admiral of the White (d. 1775). Britannia sits beside an urn holding a dipped Union flag. Behind is a stern view of one of the admiral's ships.

The monument to Thomas Spry, Admiral of the Red (d. 1828). A plinth supports a box holding naval flags, weapons and trophies. On either side a young sailor holds a rope and a young woman holds a ship's rudder.

of the stern of one of the admiral's ships is carved in low relief. The monument to Richard's nephew Thomas is alongside, the grandest in the church. He was appointed Admiral of the Red in 1805 shortly after taking part in the Battle of Trafalgar and died in 1828. (The colours red, white and blue were used at this time to denote grades of admirals.) An octagonal box standing on a plinth holds a variety of flags, naval weapons and battle trophies. To the left a barefoot young sailor holds a coil of rope while to the right a scantily clad girl holds a ship's rudder. The memorial to Gwavas May Spry who died in 1955 brings the sequence to an end. It represents a different world with different social attitudes and no doubt different finances to that of the admirals but in its simple dignity it does no discredit to the twentieth century.

When Admiral Thomas Spry died in 1828 he was succeeded by his son Samuel aged twenty-four years. He was elected M.P. for Bodmin, received a knighthood and became a leading county grandee. In 1840 he rebuilt The Place in the austere neo-Gothic style we see today. The church was then in very poor condition and Samuel embarked on a major restoration guided by his cousin, who was rector of nearby St Just-in-Roseland. The site of the former chancel had become a chicken run. This was rebuilt from the ground up on the original foundations using materials to match the rest of the building. Two granite coffins were found near the high altar, the skeletons within presumably those of senior canons. The latter were reburied and the coffins left exposed in the churchyard. The central crossing tower was rebuilt and given a broach spire of similar

LEFT *The mid-twentieth-century monument to Gwavas May Spry (d. 1955) represents a society very different from that of the admirals but it holds its own with simple dignity.*

BELOW *The stone coffin of a medieval prior disinterred from beneath the ruined chancel when it was rebuilt in 1850.*

design to the one on the house. The nave was re-roofed, given new furnishings and re-floored with Minton tiles. As a result the interior as a whole has an unmistakably Victorian appearance, but all this work undoubtedly saved the church.

The church was largely supported by the generosity of the Spry family for the remainder of the nineteenth century and much of the twentieth. Eventually in our own time the burden of maintaining a remote church in a parish with a tiny population became too great and it passed to the Trust in 1991.

Those who are able to do so should take the footpath that goes past the church and follow it in a complete circle on top of the cliffs around the headland where there are magnificent views of the surrounding bays.

There is a triple magic in this part of Roseland – the magic of the name, the magic of the secretive church with its reminders of monks and admirals and the surrounding magic of Cornwall's creeks, cliffs, headlands and wildlife.

8. ST JOHN THE BAPTIST, INGLESHAM, WILTSHIRE

SAXON TO GEORGIAN CRAFTSMANSHIP LOVED BY WILLIAM MORRIS

The chapel-like building dates from the years around 1200.

INGLESHAM IS ABOUT A MILE SOUTH of the market town of Lechlade at the end of a cul-de-sac lane off the road to Swindon. Whatever village or hamlet existed here in the Middle Ages has disappeared except for the church and three houses grouped around it. St John's is small enough to look more like a chapel than a parish church. There was a Saxon settlement here in *c.*950 when it was referred to in documents as Inggeneshamme, which means 'enclosure or river meadow of a man called Ingen'. There is no external architectural evidence for a Saxon church but there is a clear indication inside. The present building has a chancel projecting very slightly from the nave, prominent south porch and just a bellcote at the west end. The limestone walls are rendered externally with a cream finish. The church dates from *c.*1200 which is the transition point in England between Norman and Gothic

architecture. The south doorway within the porch is late Norman. The windows are Gothic of the early and mid-thirteenth century.

Despite its size, the nave has both north and south aisles. The arcades separating them from the nave reflect the crossover of styles. On the south side the arches are round-headed but on the north side they are pointed. The capitals on the piers have stiff-leaf foliage, an early Gothic motif (page 49). In the chancel, however, the blank arcading on the side walls is Norman. But earlier than any of this is a remarkable late Saxon sculpture on the chancel wall showing a Madonna and Child with the finger of God above pointing to His Son. The bodies are in profile but the heads are in full face and the child's legs are pulled up high. It has been suggested that the work derives from seventh-century Northumbrian sources (page 26).

The woodwork spans an unusually wide period of time. The screens are fifteenth century while the pulpit and tester are Elizabethan. The box pews in the nave and the holy table and communion rails in the chancel are seventeenth century. The box pews in the chancel for the families of rector and squire are eighteenth century. The large collection of wall paintings, which even extends to the porch, is even more wide-ranging, from thirteenth-century pictures to eighteenth- and early-nineteenth-century scriptural texts.

William Morris (1834–96), who lived at Kelmscott Manor about 3 miles to the east, had a special love of this church, and this is recorded on a wall tablet. Morris, who hated the growing amount of mass-produced, machine-made household furnishings of the late Victorian period was inspired by places like Inglesham church to initiate the Arts and Crafts Movement to promote the personal design and and manufacture of such things as furniture, fabrics, wallpaper, glass and books by skilled craftsmen. He also deplored the drastic and insensitive restorations of medieval churches by contemporary churchmen and he founded the Society for the Protection of Ancient Buildings to fight against the widespread destruction of ancient architecture and furnishings that these restorations brought about. The society funded and supervised sensitive conservation work at Inglesham in 1888–9. Morris's ideals and work were therefore early forerunners of those of the Churches Conservation Trust and the survival of this historic place is a monument to both him and it. The church was vested in the Trust in 1981.

ABOVE *The round-headed doorway is still of the Norman type. Above is one of the numerous wall texts throughout the church.*

BELOW *The north wall of the chancel has round-headed blank arcading. The box pews here are for the families of rector and squire.*

LEFT *The north aisle arcade has pointed Gothic arches and stiff-leaf capitals. The pulpit is Elizabethan and the box pews are seventeenth century.*

BELOW LEFT *A late Saxon sculpture of Madonna and Child. Above, the finger of God points down to His Son.*

BELOW RIGHT *The chancel has a seventeenth-century holy table and communion rails. The wall behind is covered with paintings of various dates.*

9. ALL SAINTS, WEST STOURMOUTH, KENT

CATHEDRAL MASONS IN OASTHOUSE COUNTRY

THE VILLAGE OF WEST STOURMOUTH in north-east Kent, halfway between Canterbury and Ramsgate, is as well hidden as any. A country lane leaving the main road reaches the village a few miles further on before ending close to the River Stour. There is no passing traffic in West Stoumouth. People come here because they want to be here. The name of the village was once more accurate than it is now. It used to be at the mouth of the River Stour where it joined the sea opposite the Isle of Thanet when the latter was a real island in the Middle Ages. When the intervening

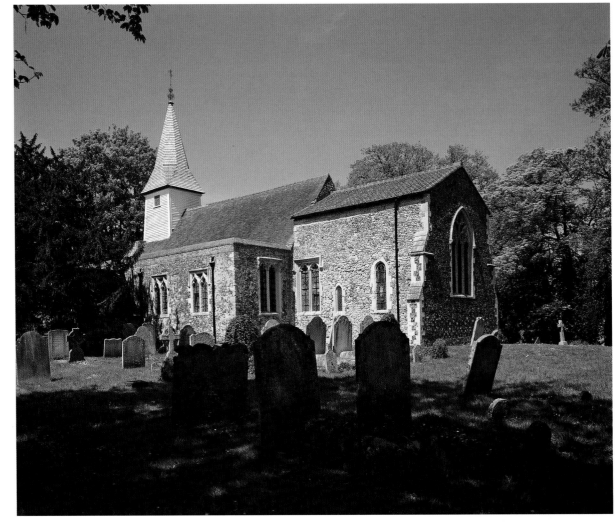

ABOVE *A symbol of Kent: an oasthouse next to the church.*

RIGHT *Most of the church dates from the late-twelfth to late-fourteenth century. It is built of local flint with limestone dressings. The tower and spire have weatherboarding and shingles.*

channel silted up and the land was reclaimed for farming Thanet was no longer an island and West Stourmouth became landlocked about 5 miles from the coast.

The church is about half a mile beyond the main group of houses of the modern village. A few fine eighteenth-century houses and a rectory are the only near neighbours at the entrance to the large tree-lined churchyard. A short distance away, an oasthouse is the archetypal symbol of rural Kent. The church has clear evidence of a Saxon predecessor in some masonry and one of the windows. This is not surprising since it is close to where St Augustine landed at Ebbsfleet from Rome in AD 597 to bring the Christian message to the Saxons. Six hundred years earlier the conquering Roman army had landed at nearby Richborough. People who shaped history entered England near this place. The present building consists of chancel, nave and aisles. A weather-boarded tower sits on the west gable with a shingled spire above. Kent, like much of east and south-east England, is chalk country and chalk goes with flint, the ubiquitous building stone in churches and secular buildings in towns and country. Apart from the limestone at corners and windows the church is built of local knapped (split) flint in pieces which are variously grey or black. In the churchyard there are a number of 'hog-backed' tombstones which are characteristic of south-east England.

The earliest part of the church is the arcade between the nave and the south aisle. It may pass unnoticed by many visitors but for architectural historian Nikolaus Pevsner this was the most memorable part of the church. It was built in c.1180, which caught the very moment that fully developed Gothic architecture first arrived in England from northern France. The Early English form of the style was created at Canterbury Cathedral in the 1170s under the direction of French masons. One of the characteristic decorative features of Early English is 'stiff-leaf' on pier capitals (see West Walton, page 47). At West Stourmouth, 'this is not

ABOVE *Eighteenth-century hog-backed gravestones in the churchyard. They are characteristic of south-east England.*

LEFT *The arcade between nave and south aisle was built in the 1180s. The Early English Gothic 'stiff-leaf' decoration on the capitals of the piers is among the first to appear in any parish church. It may have been carved by masons working at nearby Canterbury Cathedral, where the style was created.*

some rustic approximation, but boldly handled with crockets at the corners and upright leaves in between'. The work may have been done by French masons on their way to or from Canterbury. Much of the rest of the church was rebuilt in the late fourteenth century after an earthquake.

The church escaped the Victorian restorers, so most of its furnishings, except for the seventeenth-century pulpit, are of the eighteenth and nineteenth centuries. The box pews at the west end have pretty papier-mâché decoration applied to the outer sides in a very unusual way. The Royal Arms of George III hang at the west

ABOVE LEFT *The Royal Arms of George III. The Hanoverian emblems appear in the fourth (bottom right) quarter.*

ABOVE RIGHT *Papier mâché decoration applied to nineteenth-century box pews is an unusual feature.*

BELOW *A rector who reigned here for forty-three years from 1840 designed a number of rustic stained-glass windows.*

end of the south aisle. Formerly, they would probably been in a more prominent postion above the chancel arch to remind people of the Supreme Governor of the Church of England. After the death of Queen Victoria this visual emphasis was gradually reduced in churches. Long-serving Victorian rectors often liked to leave a personal mark on their churches, often financed by themselves. The Reverend Richard Drake, who was the incumbent here for forty-three years from 1840, designed several rustic looking stained glass windows.

In the 1970s the need for extensive repairs could not be met by the parishioners. After closure in 1976, vandalism and further decay left the church in a bad state. The Trust accepted responsibilty in 1980 and carried out all necessary conservation work. An active group of Friends sponsors a monthly service during the summer.

10. HOLY TRINITY, GOODRAMGATE, YORK

A SECRET ENCLAVE IN A BUSY CITY CENTRE

Dating from the thirteenth to the fifteenth century, the building is hidden in an enclosed churchyard in the centre of York. The west towers of the Minster are visible in the background.

In addition to the great Minster church, there are today nineteen medieval churches within the medieval walls of York. Based on the population in the late fifteenth century this is about one church for every 500 people. Several of the churches are less than 100 yards apart, which is of course far more than is required at the present time. As a result some are now used as cafés (and very attractive places to eat homemade food surrounded by ancient glass and monuments), some are museums of local history and a few have less dignified uses as storehouses. Many thankfully are still in active parochial use.

Just one of the nineteen, Holy Trinity, Goodramgate, is in the care of the Trust. (There is additionally one church tower.) The suffix '-gate' occurs frequently in the city. It is derived from the Old Norse *gata*, meaning a street. After the Viking

RIGHT *The chancel east window of 1470. Centre light: the Holy Trinity with the Father holding the Son and the Holy Spirit shown above as a dove. Side lights, left to right: St George with lance; St John the Baptist dressed in a camel skin; St John the Divine with chalice; St Christopher carrying the infant Christ.*

BELOW *The north aisle east window is a blaze of gold. Left: the Virgin Mary 'clothed in the garments of the sun'. Right: an archbishop similarly clothed.*

OPPOSITE ABOVE *The chancel window (detail): the three Persons of the Holy Trinity crown the Virgin Mary as Queen of Heaven.*

OPPOSITE BELOW *The church retains all of its late-seventeenth- and early-eighteenth-century woodwork: box pews stained dark brown, pulpit and altar furnishings.*

'Great Army' conquered much of northern and eastern England in the mid-ninth century, York (Yorvik) became the centre of a Viking kingdom and remained so for about 100 years. Although the church is in the heart of the city only a short distance from the Minster, it still contrives to hide itself away like so many of the Trust's rural churches. It is unusual in the city in having its own churchyard, which is entered through late Georgian iron gates and a narrow passageway between buildings. The houses and some medieval cottages which surround it on all sides create an enclave of calm away from the bustle of the shops, restaurants and old inns beyond.

The church developed in a typically piecemeal way from a Norman building of which only a few fragments survive. From

the early thirteenth century onwards aisles were added, then various chantry chapels and in the late fifteenth century a new chancel. As a result the church is a mixture of Decorated and Perpendicular Gothic with a limited amount of Victorian restoration. The churches of the city of York possess one of the finest collections of medieval glass to be seen anywhere in Europe, despite the fact that much has been destroyed deliberately, accidentally or by weathering. The Minster of course has the greater part and maintains a renowned team of research workers and craftsmen to maintain both its own glass and that sent to it from around the country. Several of the parish churches also have outstanding collections. At Holy Trinity the large five-light window in the chancel was presented in 1470 by the then rector John Walker. It has clearly experienced the ravages of time but still contains much to appreciate. The central light draws attention to the church's dedication to the Holy Trinity. In the upper part God the Father is shown holding the crucified Christ who wears a blood-stained robe. The Holy Spirit appears above them as a dove. In the lower half of the light the three Persons of the Holy Trinity crown the Virgin Mary as Queen of Heaven. Saints surround these in the side lights. At the east end of the north aisle the window is a blaze of gold. At the top the Virgin Mary is 'clothed in the garments of the sun' (Book of Revelation, 12:1) and alongside her an archbishop is similarly clothed, possibly representing the Church.

The church escaped a major Victorian restoration and so retains its early

eighteenth-century box pews which have been stained dark brown. The remaining woodwork is either late-seventeenth or early-eighteenth century, including the altar reredos, communion rails which project semi-circularly in the centre and the pulpit. The large flagstones help to retain the ancient character of the interior.

It may be well hidden, but the church attracts a large number of the millions of tourists of many nationalities who visit this most historic of English cities each year to see its Roman, Saxon, Norman, medieval and eighteenth-century architecture. As a result Holy trinity is perhaps the most visited of all the Trust's churches. It was vested in the Trust in 1972.

11. ALL SAINTS, THEDDLETHORPE ALL SAINTS, LINCOLNSHIRE

GRANDEUR AND RUSTICITY IN LONELY COASTAL MARSHLAND

THE NORTH-EAST CORNER OF LINCOLNSHIRE contains two very contrasting geographical and geological regions. To the west there are the Lincolnshire Wolds, described as resembling great frozen sea swells with their continuous low undulations. This is Jurassic limestone country, reflected in the silver-grey stone of many of the churches, the greatest of which is St James's, Louth, with its peerless steeple, the tallest of any parish church in England. To the east, between the Wolds and the North Sea, is the Lincolnshire Marshland. This, like the better known Fens to the south, is as flat as any land can be, subject over the centuries to constant flooding and so criss-crossed by innumerable dykes cutting across the land as straight as arrows like many of the roads running along beside them. When drained in this way over time the marsh has produced rich fertile land for grazing and crop cultivation. Most visitors to the area probably come for the coastal resorts, such as Mablethorpe and Skegness, and for the many miles of continuous wide lonely beaches. But for church explorers, the Marsh, like the Fens to the south, has an abundance of fine medieval churches. Prosperity from agriculture created these churches but the villages for which they were built have declined in size since the Middle Ages, or even disappeared entirely. The result is that many of the Marshland churches now stand among only half a dozen houses, or even entirely alone. Their external appearance is very different from those in the Wolds or elsewhere in the county. Not only do the contours change in dropping down from the Wolds, but so does the underlying geology. Parallel to the coast runs a broad band of chalk that is too soft for building, but further inland there is a narrower parallel band of greensand. This is a sandstone mixed with a significant amount of glauconite, a clay-like mineral containing iron silicate that gives the stone its unusual green colour. Like metallic iron, glauconite can 'rust' to a deep brown. Its presence with the sand creates an extremely friable stone which weathers badly where exposed on the surface but in the absence of a local alternative it has been extensively used in building on the Marshland. As a result, the exterior wall surfaces of the churches are weather beaten and crumbling, the effect of which can be picturesque for visitors but a headache for those who care for them. A patch-up and make-do policy has been adopted for centuries by repairers, who have used pieces of harder limestone and brick, the latter now attractively mellowed, to fill in decayed parts. The result is a patchwork quilt of building materials making rusticity rather than urbanity the sign manual of Marshland churches.

There are many cases of lonely churches without villages to support them and their clergy, and which require continuous expenditure on their fabric externally and internally, becoming redundant all over the Marsh. As a result, an exceptionaly large number has passed to the care of the Trust. Within 10 miles of Louth it presently has no fewer than nine churches.

All Saints, Theddlethorpe All Saints, just a few miles from the coast, is typical of a many of them:

The pictorial parish sign outside the churchyard features its church and the wheat which has always been a source of its wealth. Modern activity is shown by the distribution plant for natural gas coming in from the North Sea.

in size, in remoteness and in external appearance and furnishings. The parish now has no village at all; its few houses stand alone or in groups of two or three scattered among its wheat fields and vegetable crops. A church should stand out in this type of flat landscape but like so many local buildings, church or domestic, All Saints is completely ringed by trees as tall as itself, as though sheltering from the east winds that blow in from the North Sea. Furthermore, although it stands close to a minor road, its position on a sharp, S-bend means that the attention of those driving a car is distracted and it can easily be missed. Its only two companions, an eighteenth-century Hall and the former Victorian rectory, are similarly concealed within trees bordering extensive gardens. Only a handsome pictorial village sign in which the church features prominently alerts visitors to the presence of this village.

The churchyard is entered through a small wicket gate beneath the overhanging trees and the visitor steps into an oasis of total seclusion and secrecy. The church is large, out of all proportion to the present surrounding population. It consists of chancel, nave with aisles and a rather squat tower with a spikelet. The patchwork quality of the walls is noticed immediately. The green and brown rusted sandstone intermingles with pieces of grey limestone and brick. The latter is the earliest, of its kind made in England, probably at Hull in the fifteenth century. Documents tell that the building visible outside is all of one campaign between 1380 and 1400 but there is evidence of a much earlier church inside. Although by this time the last, Perpendiclar, phase of Gothic was generally established in England the window tracery here shows that the masons may have worked in the earlier Decorated style as the forms show a transition between the two.

The interior has the same diverse stonework as outside and appears larger then it is as only the east end of the nave has benches. Their absence at the

LEFT *The east end of the south aisle shows the friable sandstone from which the church was originally built, and the materials with which it was later patched up. There is greensand partly rusted to brown, silver-grey limestone and late medieval brickwork.*

RIGHT *The west end of the interior has a special sense of space created by the absense of benches.*

west end creates a special sense of space circulating around the arcade piers beteen nave and aisles. The height is also impressive because of the steeply pitched original roof. Both the aisles have chapels at their east ends. The one on the south side has a stone reredos-cum-niche whose ornate sumptuousness reinforces the view that the masons were fully familiar with the Decorated style. There are three good screens in the church. The rood screen separating nave from chancel is typically Perpendicular with the repeated emphasis on the vertical in the mullions of the upper tracery. The screens separating the two aisles from their chapels are especially interesting. Gothic tracery has now been replaced by early Renaissance motifs such as human faces in profile or frontal, surrounded by garlands. They are evidently pre-Reformation, probably *c*.1530. This is an early date for Italian Renaissance work in England where it appeared first in the decorative embellishment of architecture rather than in architecture itself in places connected with the royal court such

as Westminster Abbey and Hampton Court Palace. Its appearance at this time in such a remote place as Theddlethorpe speaks of some patron scholarly as well as wealthy.

In the chancel the evidence of the earlier church mentioned above is seen in the sedilia in the south wall, which are late Norman. The three seats set into the walls of medieval chancels were for the three priests who officiated at High Mass on special Sundays and feast days. The north side of the chancel is dominated by the large monument which rises the full height of the wall. It is for The Honourable Charles Bertie (d. 1727), son of the Earl of Lindsey. His house, now disappeared, was in the parish and he was churchwarden from 1720 to 1725. His bust in white marble and that of his wife, 'competent but dull', are placed on a black marble sarcophagus with a tall reredos holding family arms at the top.

All Saints is a remarkable example of grandeur and rusticity, unusual building materials, traditional and innovative

FAR LEFT *The sumptuously ornate stone reredos in the south aisle east chapel is more typical of the exuberance of Decorated Gothic than of the calm of Perpendicular.*

LEFT *The late Norman sedilia in the chancel for the three priests who would have celebrated high mass on special feast days is evidence of an earlier church here.*

furnishings with, of course, reminders of people, the great and the good, of former times who have worshipped here – all surrounded by a parish now only a ghost of what it once was. Already in the 1930s the entire population of the parish, even if they all attended would have occupied only a small fraction of the building and in 1939 the parishes of Theddlethorpe All Saints and neighbouring Theddlethorpe St Helen became a united benefice. By the end of the 1960s it was apparent that even the combined congregations could not support two churches and it was decided that only St Helen's surrounded by quite a large village would remain parochial. The last regular service at All Saints was held in November 1971 and it was handed over to the Trust in 1973. Since then the rather precarious fabric has required special care and attention and no doubt considerable expenditure. It is especially in places like this that visitors realise the debt of gratitude owed to the Trust.

ABOVE *Two fine and contrasting late medieval screens. Left: the rood screen between nave and chancel has the profusion of vertical mullions characteristic of Perpendicular Gothic tracery. Right: the screens of c.1530 to the aisle chapels have Classical Renaissance motifs, a remarkably early example of these in a remote rural area.*

RIGHT *The roof-high monument in the chancel to the Hon. Charles Bertie (d. 1727) and his wife. Son of the Earl of Lindsey, he lived in the parish and served as churchwarden.*

12. ST MARY, BADLEY, SUFFOLK

HIDDEN DOWN A MILE-LONG CART TRACK

THIS CHURCH IS PROBABLY FURTHER off-road than any other vested in the Trust. About 2 miles north of Needham Market on the road to Stowmarket, it is signposted along a rough cart track between the fields. The track is negotiable by car although the state of the ruts at any time will determine the speed. After a mile without passing any buildings, the track enters an open common to give the first glimpse of the church. It is only a glimpse because even in this remote place the church contrives to hide itself in a churchyard completely ringed by trees and high hedges. Its only neighbour is what now appears to be a large farmhouse a short distance further along the track. From outside the hedges one can already sense that this is going to be a homely, piecemeal sort of church. What is visible of the tower is silver-grey limestone below and mellowed brick above. The body of the church consists of an aisleless nave and a lower chancel of the same width. The overall rendering of the

At the end of a mile-long track from the main road, the church becomes partly visible within its screened churchyard at this point.

walls conceals flint rubblestone and chunks of a variety of other stones which probably look best in this concealed state. A church is recorded in the Domesday Survey of 1086 but no Saxon or Norman remains are visible. The plain south doorway is Early English Gothic, *c*.1200. Most of the present windows were inserted in the fifteenth century, including a particularly large one at the west end. An unexpectedly swagger monument on the south wall contrasts with the overall rusticity.

In the period of the Commonwealth under Oliver Cromwell in the seventeenth-century, Suffolk churches, particularly their interiors, suffered horrendously from the fanatical iconoclasm of the Puritans who removed or defaced anything they regarded as connected with 'popery'. Their agent in Suffolk was the notorious Captain Edward Dowsing, who kept a detailed of diary his despoliations as he and his soldiers travelled around the country. The entry for 5 February 1643 records his visit to Badley church. 'We brake down 34 superstitious pictures. Mr Dove promised to take down the rest.' Judging by the present large areas of plain glass most of these 'superstitious pictures' were probably in stained glass. In addition he records 'We took down 4 superstitious inscriptions with "ora pro nobis" ["pray for us"] and "cujus animae propitietur Deus" ["On whose souls may God have mercy"].' These are familiar Catholic invocations for the dead.

It is not surprising that the Victorians left this church alone like similarly remote churches described elsewhere. In 1874 there were only eighty-four people living in the parish, hardly enough to generate the necessary interest and finance needed for an ambitious restoration. As a result the church has a fascinating collection of benches

ABOVE *The church from the south.*

BELOW *The unpretentious exterior is unexpectedly relieved by the handsome monument on the chancel wall to a lawyer's wife who died in 1728.*

LEFT *The south doorway of c.1200 is protected by a porch which retains some of its medieval timbers. Beyond it, the nave is illuminated by the setting sun shining through the west window.*

ABOVE *The nave contains an unsual mixture of medieval benches and eighteenth-century box pews in an interior of exceptional rustic charm and peace.*

of several periods. There are fifteenth-century benches with poppyheads, simpler benches added in the seventeenth century and some eighteenth-century box pews for the wealthier. The carvings on the pulpit and the separate reading desk identify them, as Jacobean. All this old oak furniture has now mellowed to a lovely silver-grey. The roof is supported by tie-beams with king posts connecting them to the ridge. The floor is paved with stone flags and burial slabs. The light flooding in from the large windows and the charm of the old woodwork make this a wonderfully bright, welcoming and joyous interior. On one of my visits quite late on a Summer evening (the church is always open) the golden light from the setting sun shining in through the large west window was an experience not easily forgotten.

The large farmhouse close to the church is the remains of a sixteenth-century manor house which was reduced to one third of its size in 1739. After the Norman Conquest the manor of Badley was given to Earl Gilbert de Badele. In 1491 it passed by marriage to the Poley family, who held it until 1707. There was presumably an associated village here in the Middle Ages.

In the church the Poleys occupied the box pews in the chancel and they are commemorated by numerous wall tablets and floor slabs around the church. When they entertained Queen Elizabeth I at the manor house, she and a retinue of 200 are said to have made their way from the road along the straight path now known as Badley Walk which lies a little to the north of the present cart track.

Suffolk is magnificently rich in grand churches, often financed by the prosperous medieval wool trade. Enthusiastic church explorers will have visited many of them such as Long Melford, Lavenham, Woolpit, Southwold, Blythburgh and others, but in its own uniquely humble and charming way Badley church and its remote setting give as much pleasure as any of these and as many enduring memories.

By 1974 the population of the parish had dropped from eighty-four to less than forty. Because of this and the difficulty of access the church was declared redundant and vested in the Trust when the parish was combined with that of Needham Market in 1986.

13. ST LAWRENCE, EVESHAM, WORCESTERSHIRE

A RARE TRIO OF CHURCHES ON ONE SITE

THE HISTORIC CENTRE OF EVESHAM lies within a narrow loop of the River Avon which traffic enters and leaves across two handsome eighteenth-century bridges. The narrow streets are lined with elegant houses mainly of the same period now turned into shops at ground floor level. The town gives the immediate impression of bustling prosperity in an attractive environment.

The town's prosperity has its distant origins in the monastery founded by Bishop Egwin of Worcester in 714 when the area was part of the Saxon kingdom of Mercia. A riverside was always the ideal site for a monastery as it provided the monks with drinking water, fish for Fridays and during Lent and means of sanitation. After the Norman Conquest the monastery was refounded as a Benedictine house which over the centuries grew to rank fifth in England in size and wealth.

The church of All Saints was built at the same time as the Norman abbey within the walled precincts to serve as a parish church. Benedictine abbeys in towns customarily served the spiritual needs of the people either by allowing them the use of some part of the abbey church such as the nave or aisle for parish masses or by building a separate church near by. The monks preferred the latter as it preserved the peace and quiet of the abbey church. Like the abbey, All Saints was extended many times over the next 400 years.

It is not certain why a second parish church dedicated to St Lawrence was built within a few yards of All Saints in the twelfth century. It may be that the townspeople objected to the influx of pilgrims that an abbey always attracted and demanded that the visitors be given a separate church. St Lawrence's was substantially rebuilt in c.1400 in the Perpendicular Gothic style of the period.

At least one event of national importance took place near the abbey. Henry III, who reigned from 1216, angered the barons by his autocratic rule as had his father King John. Led by Simon de Montfort, Earl of Leicester, the barons eventually revolted. The armed supporters of king and barons waged a form of civil war which culminated in two major battles. In 1264 de Montfort won the Battle of Lewes in Sussex but on 14 August 1265 after

he and his soldiers had attended mass in the abbey church they were decisively defeated by Prince Edward, Henry's son in a battle outside the town.

Just before the Reformation Abbot Clement Lichfield built a magnificent detached bell tower, or *campanile*, adjacent to the north transept of the abbey church. Such structures were not uncommon at English cathedrals following the custom on mainland Europe. Lichfield's tower is one of the finest of its kind; the close-panelled walls rise to 110 feet (33.5 metres) with an open battlement above and a through-passageway below. It

RIGHT *The churches of St Lawrence (right) and All Saints (left), with the bell tower of the abbey church behind.*

ABOVE *The magnificent detached bell tower of the abbey church was built in c.1520 shortly before the abbey was dissolved by Henry VIII. To the left and right are the side walls of All Saints and St Lawrence's churches.*

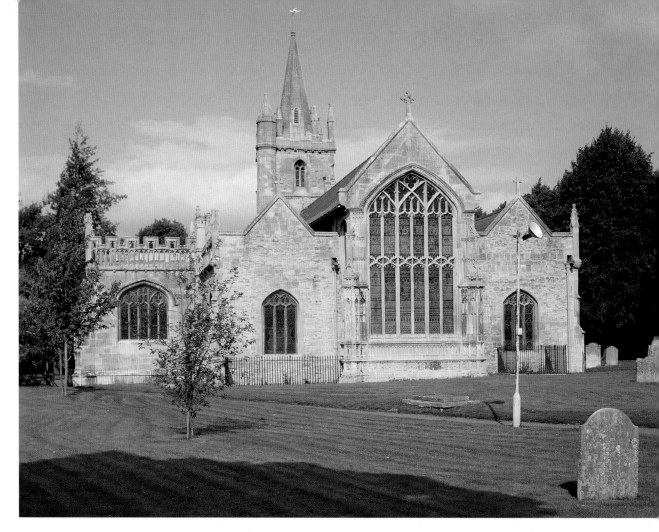

ABOVE *The east wall of St Lawrence's is filled by the large Perpendicular Gothic window.*

BELOW *The fan vault of 1513 in Abbot Lichfield's chantry chapel in St Lawrence's. Such roofs are an outstanding feature of Perpendicular architecture.*

demonstrates the pride, wealth and ambitions of some senior churchmen in the late Middle Ages. For Abbot Lichfield it was to be the pride before the fall because within a few decades the abbey was to go the way of all others when it was 'dissolved' by Henry VIII in 1540. Although the domestic quarters of the monks and the main part of the abbey church were demolished, the bell tower escaped. The result today is that there are two complete churches and one church tower within a few yards of each other.

The two churches continued in use side by side as parish churches until the 1970s serving High Church congregations (All Saints) and Low Church congregations (St Lawrence). This situation became untenable and St Lawrence's was handed over to the Trust.

St Lawrence's, like All Saints, is a large church with a chancel, aisled nave and west tower. Its large windows are typical of the Perpendicular style. At the same time that he was building the abbey bell tower, the abbot added to St Lawrence's a similarly sumptuous chantry chapel for himself adjacent to the south aisle. The roof of the chapel has a fan vault, a feature which is often regarded as the most spectacular creation of the Perpendicular style. A fan vault consists of four concave-sided inverted cones with radiating ribs which are arranged at the four corners of a bay to reach out towards the centre.

The stumpy spire was added to the west tower during one of a number of restorations in the nineteenth century. The church has a number of relics of the same period and much stained glass of the twentieth century.

In modern times the land surrounding the abbey and the churches has been well managed to the benefit of the town. The land to the north of the bell tower where the domestic quarters were situated runs down to the River Avon. This is laid out as a large open grassed area which is a favourite riverside walking place throughout the year and a picnic place in summer. The sight of swans gliding serenely by has a strangely calming effect. To the south of the bell tower the grassed area around the two churches is crossed by several paths constantly taking people from one part of the town to another.

BELOW *A nineteenth-century coffin carriage.*

BOTTOM *Modern glass in the north aisle depicts the morning of 4 August 1265, when Simon de Montfort, Earl of Leicester and his troops received Holy Communion from the abbot in the abbey church. Later in the day they were routed by the forces of Henry III at the Battle of Evesham near by.*

14. ST MARY THE VIRGIN, WIGGENHALL ST MARY THE VIRGIN, NORFOLK

THE FINEST COMPLETE SET OF MEDIEVAL BENCHES IN ENGLAND

THE FOUR WIGGENHALL VILLAGES are clustered together about 5 miles south of Kings Lynn and The Wash in the flat borderland of Norfolk and Lincolnshire. In the early Middle Ages agriculture here was not easy due to the constant flooding of the low-lying land. Drainage began under the auspices of the religious houses about 1200, and early poverty was transformed into prosperity in the late Middle Ages, a prosperity that built the great Marshland churches whose villages occur in groups – the Wiggenhalls, the Walpoles, the Tilneys and the Terringtons. No area in England has more fine churches per square mile than here.

The four Wiggenhall villages can easily be confused, particularly as they all have interesting churches. Visitors need to be careful to arrive at the desired place. There is Wiggenhall St Mary the Virgin, described here, Wiggenhall St

The large, Perpendicular Gothic church was built in c.1400. Shortly before this photograph was taken, the Trust had renewed the limewash on the walls and reroofed the building with bright red terra cotta tiles.

Mary Magdalene, Wiggenhall St Germans and Wiggenhall St Peter. The forename in each case comes from the Saxon Wigrehala, meaning 'nook of land of a man called Wicga'. All the villages are close to water in the form of river or dyke.

The church of St Mary the Virgin is about a mile outside the modern village at the end of a tree-lined cul-de-sac, where the Georgian rectory is its only companion. The large churchyard is surrounded by orchards and fields separating it from the River Ouse making its way to The Wash. It is a setting typical of many Trust churches. The church is large but its exterior is disappointing by the standards of most Norfolk churches. The walls of chancel and nave, but not the tower, are rendered and although this had been renewed shortly before my visit it can never be as attractive as mellowed stone or brick. The humble tower is too low for the tall nave and the mixture of rubblestone, stone and brick that was used shows perhaps that the rendering elsewhere is not inappropriate. A former slate roof had also been replaced recently by the Trust using bright red clay tiles which will look better when they have had a chance to mellow. The first church here was Early English Gothic of the early thirteenth century now seen only around the south door, which has a steeply pointed arch with deeply undercut multiple moldings that are characteristic of the style. Apart from this, the church was completely rebuilt in the Perpendicular Gothic period c.1400.

If the exterior of the church is disappointing, the interior is a *tour de force* of late medieval and Jacobean furnishings. The church has what is arguably the finest complete set of late medieval carved benches in England, which fills the entire nave and aisles. The original brown oak has darkened considerably with age. The benches have end pieces with niches containing carved figures, mainly saints. The

Part of the complete collection of late medieval carved benches. The ends have figures of saints below and to either side of the poppyheads above. The backs of the benches are pierced with tracery.

LEFT *Two of the fifty-eight bench ends. They have figures in the niches below and poppyheads above, with smaller figures to their left and right. Not all of the figures can be identified. Left: St Agatha. Right: Christ holding a globe.*

LEFT BELOW *Brass eagle lectern dated 1518. It is one of only about forty medieval examples surviving in England. Norfolk was a centre of their manufacture, with exports to all over Europe.*

upper part of each bench end has the familiar medieval motif of a poppyhead, a word which may derive from the Latin *puppis*, meaning the figurehead of a ship, or the French *poupée*, a doll. Very unusually, however, the poppyheads have companions in the form of much smaller carved figures one to the left and one to the right. Not all of the figures below or above can now be identified with certainty. There are no less than fifty-eight of these bench ends, of which two are illustrated above. In addition to the ends, the benches have backs with handsome pierced tracery, none of which is repeated. Curiously the benches have been dated to two periods on the basis of the dress styles of the figures. Those on the south side of the nave are *c*.1400 and those on the north side *c*.1500, but only experts will notice the divide. This woodwork must have taken a remarkable amount of skill, time, effort and expense and shows how greatly the people of the parish valued their church in the Middle Ages. The effect now is impressive if a little sombre.

The brass eagle lectern dated 1518 is only one of about forty from the Middle Ages that survive in England. East Anglia was the main centre of their manufacture and they were exported all over Europe, including one now in St Mark's Cathedral, Venice. The Wiggenhall lectern has the Latin inscription which in translation reads: 'Pray for the Soul of Master Kervile, Knight of Wiggenhall, son of Edmund Kervile of Wiggenhall, whose heart is buried here.' Thousands of lecterns of this design were replicated in the nineteenth and twentieth centuries.

(Shortly before my visit the lectern had been stolen, then recovered. It says much for the attitude of the Trust that it was not timidly transferred to the safety of a museum but was restored to its proper home, albeit now guarded by additional security.)

Of the chancel rood screen of *c*.1500, only the dado remains. The panels have paintings of saints which can be identified by their symbols.

The medieval font has a pretty Jacobean cover topped by a carving of a

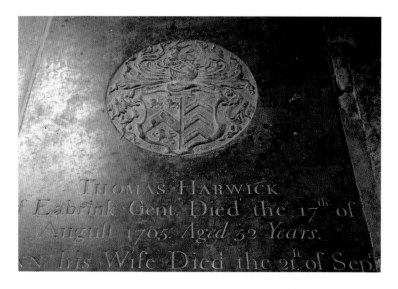

'pelican in its piety'. The bird, which was thought at the time to feed its young by pecking blood from its own breast, was used as a mystic symbol of Christ's blood in the sacrament of the eucharist.

A number of handsome slate ledger stones are let into the floor. They were popular from the mid-seventeenth to the mid-nineteenth century to commemorate prosperous gentry, professional and trades people in a parish. They generally bear a simple but finely carved inscription and a deeply incised roundel containing a coat of arms or other device of the deceased. The church was conservatively restored in the nineteenth century when such things as the stone-flagged floor were retained. As a result, the numerous fine furnishings can be seen in a fittingly dignified atmosphere.

In the twentieth century the population of the village declined. It could not provide for the upkeep of its church and since the one at Wiggenhall St Germans was only a mile away, St Mary the Virgin was declared redundant and vested in the Trust in 1982.

TOP LEFT *The dado of the rood screen of c.1500 has painted saints with their symbols. Left to right: St Mary Magdalene with a box of ointment; St Dorothy with a basket of fruit; St Margaret with a cross and dragon below; St Scholastica with a black Benedictine cowl.*

TOP *The medieval font has a seventeenth-century cover surmounted by a carving of a 'pelican in its piety', a traditional symbol of the eurcharist.*

ABOVE *One of several handsome early-eighteenth-century slate ledger stones set into the floor. They commemorate the wealthier of the parish with fine inscriptions and deeply incised roundels with family arms.*

15. WITHCOTE CHAPEL, LEICESTERSHIRE

A TUDOR GEM WITH STAINED GLASS BY A KING'S GLAZIER

WITHCOTE HALL AND CHAPEL are about 4 miles west of the little market town of Oakham in an area where a network of minor roads link several villages and hamlets. An inconspicuous and unsignposted driveway gives no indication that it leads to a handsome early Georgian house and the adjacent chapel built for its medieval predecessor. The lack of a signpost on the road and the fact that one walks just a few yards in front of the main entrance to the house in order to reach the chapel next to it may give visitors a feeling of intruding in this private place.

At the end of the fifteenth century the manor of Withcote belonged to William Smith and his wife Catherine. Their decision to build a private chapel next to their manor house may have been connected with the fact that a local thirteenth-century chapel-of-ease to the parish church at Oakham had disappeared. After William's death in 1506, Catherine and her second husband Roger Ratcliffe continued with the building which was completed c.1530. From the outset it was likely to have been used by local tenants as well as the family. The chapel has been described as a miniature version of the great collegiate chapels built around the same time by royalty and other patrons, for example King's College Chapel, Cambridge and Eton College Chapel, both started by Henry VI. Like them, the plan of Withcote chapel is a simple rectangle with no internal divisions of any kind. This sort of spatial unity was one of the ideals of the Perpendicular Gothic style of the time. The four three-light windows with round heads that fill much of the north and south sides are typically late Perpendicular Tudor. The local buff-coloured limestone is used for the main structure with a contrasting silver-grey limestone for the windows. The battlements with a decorated frieze below were added in the mid-eighteenth century.

The chapel is important because it is a very rare survival of its type and more important because of the contemporary stained glass that fills the windows. The arms of Jane Seymour, who was Henry VIII's third wife, appear in one of

The south side of the chapel, built in the early sixteenth century. Its simple rectangular plan and large windows have led it to be described as a miniature version of the contemporary King's College Chapel, Cambridge. The Hall is on the far side.

the windows and fix their date as 1536–7. The arms of the Smiths and Ratcliffes appear in others. The glass is attributed to Henry VIII's glazier Galyon Hone. He worked at Eton and King's College Chapel so he would have been familiar with the plan of the building he was glazing. The iconography of the windows was planned from the start as a unified scheme with prophets on the south side and apostles on the north. This follows a favourite idea in medieval biblical scholarship in which a 'concordance' was seen between Old Testament and New Testament characters, the work of the latter fulfilling the work of the former. The majority of the glass survived the iconcoclasm of the Reformation which broke out all over England so shortly after the glass was installed and also that of the Puritans during the Cromwellian Commonwealth in the next century. However, not all the glass is now in its original position. A selection of the glass is shown.

Tudor glass.

ABOVE LEFT *From left to right: the prophets Amos, Micah and Zephaniah. Note the Tudor Royal Arms and other symbols in the upper lights.*

ABOVE RIGHT *From left to right: the prophet Zachariah, and the apostles Jude and Thomas with a spear.*

BELOW LEFT *From left to right: the apostles John, Andrew with cross and Peter with keys.*

BELOW RIGHT *St Philip (left) and St James (right).*

In the early eighteenth century the estate was bought by Matthew Johnson whose son Geoffrey demolished the old manor house and built the present Hall *c.*1730. It is 'a plain reasonable, cream-coloured and extremely lovable house' writes Pevsner in a rare display of personal affection.

The new owners completely remodelled the interior of the chapel. The chancel has a reredos 'in a noble Wren style'. The centre of the three sections has two columns on either side of a copy of a painting of *The Two Trinities* by Murillo. It shows Mary and Joseph as one group and God the Father land the Holy Spirit as another group linked together by the infant Christ. The two side sections of the reredos are canted out to act as frames for two white marble monuments to Matthew and Geoffrey Johnson, above. In the nave the walls were lined with stalls facing inwards and backed by panelling, all in the same dark wood as the reredos. The floor was paved with white and black marbles. The interior is thus equally divided between the medieval and the Classical. The centre of the nave has a number of incongruous early twentieth century

benches unworthy of the chapel. Outside it is puzzling why a tall conifer hedge screens off the chapel from the Hall. This handsome small building would surely enhance the view from the principal windows of any house.

In the 1970s services were held here only once a month with a congregation of only three or four people and as a result the chapel was vested in the Trust in 1979.

16. ST NINIAN, BROUGHAM, CUMBRIA

WITNESS TO THE ENERGY OF A REDOUBTABLE SEVENTEENTH-CENTURY COUNTESS

THE VILLAGE OF BROUGHAM is about 2 miles south-east of Penrith on the main road to Appleby. The road passes through the exhilaratingly open, rolling hills characteristic of the Scottish border country. When travelling eastwards, the much higher ridge of the Pennines can be seen in the distance and when westwards the high Cumbrian mountains. The road now bypasses the village but its castle is a prominent landmark for travellers. Like most of its kind it is now ruined though a very substantial and magnificent ruin. In places it rises through four storeys to a height of about 80 feet. It was built during the reign of Henry II (1154–89) as a royal fortress guarding against Scottish raids. In the late thirteenth century the castle passed by marriage to the Clifford family, Earls of Cumberland and great landowners in the area, about whom more presently.

Continuing for about a mile in the direction of Appleby, only very observant motorists will notice a field gate set back a little from the road on the northern side and beside it a small wooden signpost pointing away across the fields. There is just room to park a car here and to see that the sign directs walkers to 'Ninekirks'. This is the local name for the church of St Ninian, reflecting the proximity to Scotland where St Ninian lived and worked as a missionary in the fourth century in the south of the country. There is no building in sight as the rough track leads across the fields and shortly comes to the River Eamont, a tributary of the River Eden, whose fast-flowing waters have cut a deep bed that reveals the local New Red Sandstone in its banks. This is a lovely warm-coloured sandstone paricularly in bright sunlight. As the visitor might start to wonder about the whereabouts of a church the track rises slightly and from the brow of the incline there is a remarkable sight. Ahead a low, ground-hugging church of red sandstone lies in the middle of a field surrounded by a fenced, overgrown churchyard with not another building in sight. Closer up, among the eighteenth- and nineteenth-century gravestones, it can be seen that the architecture is all of one style and that the round-headed windows under square hood-moulds and the priest's door into the chancel all tell of the mid-seventeenth century. This is a form of

TOP *Brougham Castle, one of the ancestral homes of Lady Anne Clifford, the builder of St Ninian's church. She died here in 1676.*

ABOVE *About a mile from the nearest road, this is the first glimpse that visitors have of St Ninian's, totally alone among the Cumbrian fells.*

The architectural details tell of the mid-seventeenth century.

'Gothic Survival', favoured by conservative patrons at the time: a restrained form of medieval Gothic with Classical overtones.

Everything in the interior matches the mid-seventeenth-century date outside. Structurally and in its furnishings it is clearly in the same untouched condition as in the year it was made. The interior is a single rectangular room, the aisleless nave and the chancel have no structural division between them. Everything contributes to a sense of cool, calm dignity in which nothing is out of place. The floor is made of massive stone flags, everything else is either white or brown. The walls are rendered and whitewashed as is the ceiling. All else is wood: the smoothly planed box pews and the rougher timbers of the roof above. At the front of the church there are two family pews much taller than the rest of the so-called 'horse-box' type with balusters in the Jacobean way. The communion rails have the dumb-bell form of the later seventeenth century. The altar reredos, pulpit and stone font are of the same time. To the side of the studded oak door there is a contemporary iron poor-box in which the money drops down a pillar for the sake of safety. Evidently

pilfering was as much a problem then as now. Above it on the wall hangs an eighteenth-century funeral hatchment which gives one of the few restrained splashes of colour to the interior. These memorials of an aristocratic death are quite common in Trust churches but rare elsewhere.

Most visitors will now be wondering why such a church was built in such a remote place, apparently for the first time in the seventeenth century. The period was not one of great church building in England. The huge legacy of medieval churches and the religious strife following the Reformation for several generations saw to that. The answer to the question can be found in two features in the church; those high family pews which tell of someone of rank and the letters AP moulded in plaster beside the altar, surrounded by a garland. The whole of the land around here and much beyond was the property of the Clifford family, Earls of Cumberland. The 3rd Earl, George Clifford (1558–1605), married Margaret Russell, daughter of the Earl of Bedford, and they had a daughter, Lady Anne Clifford, born in 1590. The Earl left the countess some time after Anne's

The interior is still exactly as furnished in 1650. It has a cool, restrained dignity reflecting the wealth and taste of its patron.

birth and thereafter mother and daughter had a pariculary close relationship. At the age of nineteen Lady Anne married Richard Sackville, Earl of Dorset, who died in 1624. Her mother had died in 1616. Anne married secondly Philip Herbert, Earl of Pembroke and Montgomery, who in turn died in 1650, leaving Anne a widow for the second time at the age of sixty. Neither of these marriages had been successful by her own account. Anne had been lonely and unhappy living in great houses so far from home. By this time Henry Clifford, the 5th Earl of Cumberland, had died without issue in 1643, and Anne inherited the vast estates of the family in Cumberland, Westmorland and Yorkshire. After the death of her second husband she travelled north to claim the properties using the grandiloquent titles of Lady Anne Clifford, Dowager Countess of Dorset, Pembroke and Montgomery, At the age of sixty (then a greater age than now) a quiet retirement might have seemed in order but that was not in her nature. In the event she was to live for another twenty-six years and she devoted it untiringly to two passionate causes. The first involved repairing or even rebuilding the family

castles and parish churches on her estates that had fallen into disrepair or near dereliction. Stone, brick and mortar were now the materials of her life. The second was based on an immense family pride which led to a preoccupation in claiming for herself through the courts several ancestral titles, mainly baronies subsidiary to the earldom that accrued to the Cliffords over the centuries but which had gone into abeyance. Following the repair of her homes it became her custom to spend fixed time of the year at each of her six castles: Brougham, Appleby, Brough, Pendragon, Skipton and Barden, the last two being in West Yorkshire. All this might imply an extravagant lifestyle. In fact she had a frugal personal way of living regarding food, clothing and travelling. Most of her wealth not taken up in building operations was dispensed in charity to friends and relatives. It must be remembered that all this was taking place during one of the most troubled periods of English history: the conflict between Charles I and Parliament followed by the Civil War and the Commonwealth under Cromwell. Lady Anne was an outspoken supporter of the king against the parliament and

LEFT *The family pews for Lady Anne and her household are of the 'horse-box' type.*

ABOVE *The dumb-bell balusters of the communion rails.*

RIGHT *The seventeenth-century pillar-type poor box, which prevented pilfering, and the eighteenth-century funeral hatchment beside the studded oak door.*

of the High Church party against the Puritans when it was a dangerous time for such outspokenness. So we get the picture of an extremely feisty old lady with prodigious physical energy and immense ambitions and willpower.

This is the person we must have in mind as we stand inside this remote and highly atmospheric little church among the Cumbrian fells. When she returned north in 1650 she found at Brougham a medieval church in poor condition. She wrote in her diary: 'It [Ninekirks] would in all likelihood have fallen down it was soe ruiness if it had not bin repaired by me.' In the Middle Ages Ninekirks was the parish church of Brougham but some time before 1400 a chapel-of-ease was built near the castle which gradually became the main place of worship. Ninekirks was used less and fell into disrepair. The rebuilding (for such it was) was carried out 1650–1 and has never been altered since, outside or inside except for the south porch added in the nineteenth century. A well preserved seventeenth-century parish church is a very special survival for the reasons mentioned. The quality but quiet restraint of all the furnishings indicates a patron of wealth and good taste. They were designed to provide the simple, dignified setting that the High Church liked for the celebration of the liturgy at the period. We can now understand

the reason for the two tall family pews at the front of the church used by Lady Anne and her household and for the garlanded letters AP with the date 1660. They stand for Anne Pembroke. She never failed to leave a discreet but reasonably prominent reminder to posterity of her restorations of churches and castles. Few churches in England are as remote and secret. I have visited nearly 2,000 English churches at an estimate, and Brougham remains among the five most memorable because of its setting, its architecture, its furnishings and its associations with a remarkable lady. Whatever village was around the church in the Middle Ages has long since disappeared, so that it is remarkable that the church escaped redundancy until as late as 1977.

On their way back to the road and modern life visitors may imagine a little procession of no doubt black-robed ladies with their male attendants making their way on horseback or in carriages along the same track from Brougham to morning service at the church on Sunday mornings over 300 years ago. Lady Anne died in Brougham Castle on 22 March 1676 where her father had been born and her mother had died. She is buried in Appleby church, where a large but typically restrained monument has no effigy but a tall wall plate with inevitably a large display of the coats of arms of the Cliffords, Russells and the familes into which they married.

17. ST WERBURGH OLD CHURCH, WARBURTON, GREATER MANCHESTER

A LOVABLE MUDDLE OF STONE, BRICK AND WOOD

THE VILLAGE OF WARBURTON IS CLOSE to the south bank of the upper reaches of the River Mersey. As the river has traditionally been the boundary between Lancashire and Cheshire, Warburton has been until recently a Cheshire village. That changed with the reorganisation of the county boundaries in 1974 when Manchester was separated from Lancashire and expanded on all sides to create a new county of Greater Manchester. The expansion took no account of

The early eighteenth century brick tower seen from outside the lych gate. Other parts date back to the thirteenth century.

the natural dividing line of the river and brought Warburton into the new county. Nevertheless many older residents doubtless continue to think of themselves as Cheshire people. A pre-visit check of a map of the wider area around the village may not encourage church explorers who like the scenic parts of England. The village is just south of one of the largest industrial connurbations in Europe stretching some 40 miles from Liverpool to Manchester. Warrington is only 4 miles to the west and Salford and the satellite towns of Manchester are only the same distance to the east. So on arriving it is a pleasant

surprise to find that the River Mersey acts as a northern barrier to most of that and everything on the south side of the village is Cheshire's lush dairy farmland.

The road through the village divides it into two halves, smaller modern houses on one side and larger older houses on the other. A lane that leads into the older half ends within a few hundred yards inside a circle of tall trees through which the church is enticingly visible. A former rectory on one side of the very large churchyard and a house on the other are completely screened by the trees. So despite the appearances on the maps Warburton church is as secluded and silent as others of the Trust. It was Pevsner who described it, above, as a 'lovable muddle', a muddle of materials and dates. The tower facing the lych gate is mellowed brick and confusingly is at the east, chancel end of the building rather than at the western end as usual. The south side of the church is local sandstone while the north side is timber-framed. Cheshire and the counties to the south, Shropshire and Worcestershire are noted for their timber-framed buildings but it is rare to find timber-framed churches. St Werburgh's is only one of twelve to survive in Cheshire. It is possible to be certain about some dates. The south stone wall is inscribed 1647 and the brick tower 1711. Radiocarbon dating of some of the external and internal woodwork has given a date 1250–1395. This medieval date fits in with the documentary evidence. Land deeds of 1151 for St Werburgh's Benedictine Abbey at Chester (now the cathedral) refer to abbey property at Warburton and a document of 1187 refers to a chapel here. St Werburgh, who died in *c.*700, was a Saxon princess, daughter of Wulfhere the first Christian king of Mercia. The Normans are unlikely to have chosen this dedication unless there was already a pre-existing Saxon church on the site. About 1190 Premonstratensian canons (of an order founded in Premontre in France) came to start a small priory which concentrated

on parish and missionary work rather than enclosed monastic life. The priory appears not to have prospered and it was abandoned in the mid-thirteenth century. The core of the present building may date from the time of the canons or a little later. After the departure of the canons, Warburton church was within and at least partly dependent on the nearby parish of Lymm.

Most of the exterior is stone or brick but inside the church is a forest of massive oak timbers in the lower parts as well as the roof. The aisled nave consists of two bays and the chancel of one. The timber uprights are roughly hewn octagonal pillars which mimic their contemporary stone counterparts. They carry horizontal tie-beams additionally strengthened by braces. Higher again, collar beams are supported by struts. Longitudinal purlins tie in the rafters. The whole open structure from ground level to the apex of the roof reveals exactly how the load of the superstructure is carried down to the floor.

About 1600 the chancel was refurnished. The pulpit has the characteristic blank arcading decoration of the time. The communion rails have turned balusters and surround the heavy oak altar table on three sides in the Puritan, Low Church style. Many people are buried beneath the stone-flagged floor. One of the few Victorian intrusions is the stained-glass window in the chancel, which has the benefit of providing a splash of colour in a rather sombre interior, best seen on a sunny day.

In 1880 the church was in such a bad state of repair, inevitable with this amount of structural wood, that it was decided to build another church about a quarter of a mile away across the fields — New St Werburgh's. However, this was done only on the condition of the then rector that the old church was not demolished. Between the 1880s and the 1950s a great deal of effort and money was expended in treating those two scourges of ancient woodwork: dry rot and deathwatch beetle. The church was vested in the Trust in 1971.

18. ST JOHN THE BAPTIST OLD CHURCH, PILLING, LANCASHIRE

FROM THE DAWN OF GEORGIAN CHURCH BUILDING

THE VILLAGE OF PILLING is near the north Lancashire coast in a corner of the county little visited or known even to many Lancastrians. Millions of people pass close each year on the M6 motorway making their way to Blackpool to the south or the Lake District some distance to the north. In between these Meccas of tourism the area is left to itself. The approach to the village from the motorway is across a flat marshy coastal area, where the fields are bordered by drainage ditches or deeper and wider dykes. In Lancashire marshy land is known as a 'moss' and several are named on local maps.

The church is a simple but attractive building of 1717, built without any desire for show.

They are strikingly similar to the Lincolnshire Fens and for those familiar with the distant views of the spires of the great Lincolnshire Fen churches the resemblance is heightened by the first sight of the spire of Pilling New Church when still some miles away. However, in north-west England, unlike the Fens, the mountains are never far away. Approaching the village, the Cumbrian mountains to the north are clearly visible 20 miles away across Morecambe Bay, while on the return journey to the east there are the lower hills of the Forest of Bowland about 5 miles away and beyond them the higher ridge of the Pennines closes off the horizon.

Pilling is a scattered-out village without a clear centre and little in the way of picturesque or historic buildings except the one we have come to see. The village is part of the huge parish of Garstang 6 miles away to the south. In the Middle Ages Pilling had a chapel-of-ease which was served by the monks of Cockersand Abbey about 6 miles to the north. After the Reformation the chapel remained in use served by curates until the beginning of the eighteenth century when the villagers decided it was too small and too dilapidated to repair. A new church was built in 1717. It is a moderately large building with a simple rectangular ground plan without structural division between nave and chancel. It is lit by large round-headed windows of clear glass. At the west end there is a simple doorway and a rather baroque looking bell-cote above. The lack of a tower or a pillared portico in front of the door suggests that the church was built to a budget without the help of a wealthy patron. The approach to the door across the spacious churchyard is through a yew alley planted relatively recently, a charming addition. There is a pretty sundial above the door dated 1756 with the admonitory inscription 'Thus Eternity Approacheth'. The church is built of brown sandstone with contrasting grey sandstone for the window and door surrounds.

Like Brougham church (pages 83–7) and a number of other eighteenth century churches the interior remains (except for one addition) exactly

ABOVE *The yew alley leading to the south door.*

RIGHT *The sundial of 1756 above the door warns worshippers about their final end.*

ABOVE *The interior has remained untouched from the time of building except for the gallery along the west and north side added in 1813. The plain benches and the unadorned whitewashed walls give a rather spartan effect.*

BELOW *The chancel has the seventeenth-century Puritan style arrangement of 'holy table' surrounded by communion rails on three sides. In this way there was maximum contact between minister and people during celebration of the Sacrament.*

as it was fitted up in 1717 so that the exterior and interior are a perfect period piece. The large clear glass windows flood the church with a light that is enhanced by walls painted in white. Victorian intervention, had it happened, would have resulted in probably mediocre or poor stained glass. The eighteenth century liked clarity in its churches, not the 'dim religious light' of the Middle Ages. The floor has large large stone flags which give period character to the interior. The seating consists mainly of plain dark oak benches with open backs which again indicates that the building was done on a budget. Inevitably, however, the proprieties of the time had to be observed in the form of the rather higher box pews at the front on the north side. These would have been for the rector's family, the squire and perhaps some prominent landowner. At the east end below a large window there is a typical 'Puritan' chancel arrangement. The altar is a plain 'holy table' surrounded on three sides by communion rails with handsome carved balusters. The Low Church wing of Anglicanism favoured this arrangement in place of the more usual communion rail across the full width of the chancel. In this way the minimum of separation between minister and congregation was achieved. Nothing could be further removed from the celebration of the mass before the Reformation, when the priest would be isolated from the laity at the far end of a long chancel and even sight of him would be obstructed by a tall rood screen separating chancel from nave. (Liturgical practice has gone full circle. In most Anglican and Roman Catholic churches the altar has now been brought forward to the front of the chancel or into the nave. In modern centrally planned churches the pews surround the altar in an entirely Puritan-style way.) The pulpit to the right of the chancel was originally a three-decker but at some time the lowest clerk's deck was removed. Behind on the wall are the Royal Arms of George I dated 1719 with the specifically Hanoverian part of the arms in the fourth quarter.

In 1813, just a hundred years after the church was built, it was too small for the congregations and it was decided to build a two-sided gallery down the full lenth of the north side as well as across the west end. It is supported on slender Classical style columns. The roof had to be slightly raised to allow for this and to light the gallery a row of semi-circular windows was inserted high up in the

The pulpit with the Royal Arms of George I behind, dated 1719.

north wall. With the addition of the gallery the church could now seat 350 people. The fact that the gallery was not simply for the *hoi polloi* (as the gallery in a theatre) is shown by the fact that some of the seating up here is in the form of box pews with the family names on the doors. It is an odd sensation today sitting or standing in one of those pews at the chancel end looking immediately down rather than upwards at the top deck of the pulpit. It seems that at Pilling the gallery formed what in a theatre would be the royal circle, the box pews on the ground at the front obviously the orchestra stalls while the plain benches at the back formed the pit. It is easy to imagine people in Georgian dress crowded into this church, or later in Regency times the women in crinolines and the men in wide trousers and frock coats and carrying stovepipe hats climbing up into the gallery for matins.

By 1883 the population of the village had risen to over 1,600, about twice what it had been when the gallery was added in 1813. Once again, therefore, it was decided to build a substantial new church on a site just 200 yards to the north of the old one. A handsome building of some character and originality was designed by the distinguished northern firm of Austin and Paley in the Gothic Revival style. The original intention was to demolish the eighteenth-century church but fortunately this was not done. The result, however, was that the new church was given the same dedication as the old, so that Pilling has since had an Old Church of St John the Baptist and a New Church of St John the Baptist. It is, of course, the spire of the latter that one sees on the approach to the village.

Although some maintenance work was done on the Old Church in the years that followed, by 1989 it was in a ruinous condition with parts of the roof missing. Thankfully the Trust assumed responsibilty and instigated major repairs and conservation work with total respect for the historical integrity of the building. As the photographs illustrate, the Old Church is now in perfect condition outside and inside. The two churches share the same churchyard which means that there is a steady trickle of of visitors around the Old Church as they tend family graves. That has prevented any sense of isolation that the building may otherwise have acquired. Pilling Old Church is not great architecture and its fittings and furnishings are not great art or craftsmanship. Pevsner gives it just eight lines in his North Lancashire volume. What makes it memorable to the average visitor is the way in which it remains a time capsule of a church interior, a form of churchmanship and a rural society of 300 years ago.

19. ST KATHERINE, CHISELHAMPTON, OXFORDSHIRE

A GEORGIAN 'DOLL'S HOUSE' CHURCH

THE VILLAGE OF CHISELHAMPTON is about 7 miles south-east of Oxford close to the River Thames, at the junction of two busy roads linking it the city and nearby towns. The oldest secular building is the village inn; most of the houses are modern. The church is about half a mile outside the village close to the road next to a farmhouse. It should be easy to find, but its size, some trees and a high hedge make it less obvious than expected. Many motorists travelling at speed along a straight stretch of road may pass regularly without seeing it.

LEFT *The pretty façade of 1762 is an unconventional combination of Classical elements.*

BELOW *The chancel reredos is a relatively simple example of its kind without excessive opulence.*

The estate at Chiselhampton was bought by Charles Peers a London porcelain merchant in 1760. He demolished the medieval church in 1762 and the old mansion of the Dudley family in 1768, replacing both with fashionable Classical buildings. He moved the new church to its present site on higher ground away from the river, as the old church had been liable to flooding. The old church was dedicated to St Mary. Peers changed the dedication of the new one to St Katherine, in honour of his wife. (Such was the power of the landed gentry in those times.) It is not one of the grandest types of Classical eighteenth-century churches; its interest is in its charm rather than its size. The design is attributed to Samuel Dowbiggin, a London housebuilder.

St Katherine's is a simple Georgian 'preaching box' or 'auditory' church, so called because its plain rectangular groundplan and elevation were designed at a time when the principal Sunday services in an Anglican church were matins and evensong, at which preaching was a major part. The celebration of Holy Communion could take place as little as four times a year. The charmingly petite façade of the church invites comparison with a little doll's house by which no disrespect is intended. The brickwork with stone dressings is rendered in white and the lower part of the façade is quite plain. The central doorway has only a simple decorative moulding. The gable has urns at its base to left and right. Higher up it is more ornate. Small volutes at the apex of the gable lead to a wooden clock-turret. This is continued upwards with an open-sided turret which is topped with a weathervane. The composition may not conform to the canons laid down for a Classical façade but it provides a pretty, cheerful face to the building nonetheless.

The interior is well lit by the large round-headed clear glass windows on the south side. It retains the complete set of original fittings, which creates the coolly elegant dignity that eighteenth-century Anglicans liked. Behind the plain holy table in the chancel, a large tripartite reredos covers the east wall. It is a good design well carved without the ornateness that might be seen in contemporary London churches. The gilded panels are inscribed with the Commandments, Creed and Lord's Prayer, as

required by law at the time. The central panel is raised above the others by a segmental pediment. The altar rails have twisted balusters.

Box pews fill the nave either side of the centre aisle, the ones to the front for the Peers family and the rector's family a little higher than those behind to emphasise the stratification of society. The three-decker pulpit is Jacobean, presumably taken from the old church. It is placed against the north wall in the centre of the church rather than near the altar, which was not uncommon in Low Church practice. It certainly helps the preacher in making this an 'auditory' church but with the odd result that he is speaking to the backs of half of his congregation. (Seats on two or three sides of box pews could sometimes allow people to face either way during services). The prominent chandeliers are nineteenth century. Pevsner describes the font as a plain marble 'pudding basin' on a wooden base.

The parishioners commissioned a major restoration of the church 1952–4. The modern stained-glass window showing the arms of the Peers family was inserted at this time. John Betjeman, who later was to write many church poems (now published in their own volume) and was to become Poet Laureate, 'turned' some verses in aid of this restoration (opposite).

The church did not 'fall', thanks to the efforts of the parishioners but in the 1970s the upkeep of the church became too onerous for local people and it was handed over to the Trust in 1978.

ABOVE *The three-decker pulpit is placed against the centre of a side wall to assist audibility in this 'preaching box' church.*

RIGHT *The font is a plain marble 'pudding bowl' on a wooden base.*

FAR RIGHT *Stained glass of 1954 shows the arms of the Peers family, who built the church in 1762.*

VERSES TURNED
in aid of A PUBLIC SUBSCRIPTION

TOWARDS THE RESTORATION OF THE CHURCH OF
ST KATHERINE,
CHISELHAMPTON, OXON.

Across the wet November night
The church is bright with candlelight
And waiting Evensong.
A single bell with plaintive strokes
Pleads louder than the stirring oaks
The leafless lanes along.

It calls the choirboys from their tea
And villagers, the two or three,
Damp down the kitchen fire,
Let out the cat, and up the lane
Go paddling through the gentle rain
Of misty Oxfordshire.

How warm the many candles shine
On SAMUEL DOWBIGGIN'S design
For this interior neat,
These high box pews of Georgian days
Which screen us from the public gaze
When we make answer meet;

How gracefully their shadow falls
On bold pilasters down the walls
And on the pulpit high.
The chandeliers would twinkle gold
As pre-Tractarian sermons roll'd
Doctrinal, sound and dry.

From that west gallery no doubt
The viol and serpent tooted out
The Tallis tune to Ken,
And firmly at the end of prayers
The clerk below the pulpit stairs
Would thunder out 'Amen'.

But every wand'ring thought will cease
Before the noble altarpiece
With carven swags array'd,
For there in letters all may read
The Lord's Commandments, Prayer and Creed
Are decently display'd.

On country mornings sharp and clear
The penitent in faith draw near
And kneeling here below
Partake the Heavenly Banquet spread
Of Sacramental Wine and Bread
AND JESUS' presence know.

And must that plaintive bell in vain
Plead loud along the dripping lane?
And must the building fall?
Not while we love the Church and live
And of our charity will give
Our much, our more, our all.

JOHN BETJEMAN

20. ST ANDREW, SHOTLEY, NORTHUMBERLAND

IN PROMINENT ISOLATION ON A MOORLAND HILLTOP

VISITORS TO BYWELL (pages 26–8) would pass within half a mile of Shotley church if coming from the south and would need to make only a short detour if coming from other directions. Although they are close together, the immediate surroundings of the two churches could hardly be more different. Bywell is hidden in a lush river valley; Shotley isolated on a bare hilltop overlooking the Bishop Aukland to Corbridge road. About 5 miles south of Bywell where the road is still high above the Tyne valley, a minor road leads up to the broad flat top of Grey Mare Hill about half a mile away. From the main road only those looking for it are likely to see a small low building standing alone on the hilltop just visible on the skyline. Remarkably this has been the site of a parish church for several hundred years. The road uphill brings visitors to a field gate, the nearest point to the church accessible by car. The church is now visible across a field. A 200-yard tramp along the resemblance of a footpath at the side of the field leads to the entrance of the stone-walled churchyard. On wet ground heavy shoes or boots are advisable. (Funerals in the past must have been a problem for the coffin bearers and would still be so today.) A stone farmhouse some distance away is the only neighbour. From the churchyard there are panoramic views for 5 miles or more to the west and south across treeless moorland.

ABOVE *The church as seen from the east at the start of the footpath, which is the only access to it around a field. To the right, the remarkable Hopper monument in the churchyard is higher than the church.*

BELOW *A close view of the cruciform church built in 1764 in a simple Classical style. The view to the western horizon byond stretches for miles across Northumberland moorland.*

The present building was erected in 1769 to replace a medieval church. Unless there was still a village here at the time of rebuilding it is strange that the new church was erected on the same site. It has a cruciform plan, reflecting no doubt the Georgian love of symmetry and antique precedents even in such a small and humble building as this. There is hardly any vertical accent except for a tiny pedimented bell-cote at the west end. The church may be unremarkable architecturally but not so the presence of the large mausoleum in the churchyard. It was built by Humphrey Hopper in 1752 for his wife. Hopper was the head of the wealthy local family who had financed the building of the new church. He joined his wife in the mausoleum in 1756, later followed by their children and grandchildren. It is a complex structure made up of Classical elements but with none of the discipline associated with Classical architecture. It has a square

ground plan, the base containing a recess for the recumbent effigies of Hopper and his wife. Above this on each side are seated figures in niches with a cornice above supported by columns. Standing on this is a square dome with obelisks at the corners and higher again an open lantern with obelisks. The effect is more Baroque than Classical. It would catch the eye even in Highgate and Kensal Green cemeteries in London; up here on an isolated northern hilltop it seems bizarre. However, as we have seen elsewhere in this book, the eighteenth-century aristocracy and gentry always wanted to be commemorated in their rural parish churches, however remote they were. In extreme contrast, there are several gravestones of the humblest kind representing people at the other end of the social spectrum. Some scarcely rise above the long grass but not inconsiderable amounts must have been paid to some local artisan mason. Between 1769 and the building of a more accessible church lower down the valley in 1836 it must have required considerable commitment and energy to attend services at Shotley church. It was vested in the Trust in 1973.

LEFT *The large Hopper family monument is an extraordinary sight alongside a small church in such a remote place. The design is a complex Baroque combination of several Classical elements.*

BELOW *By contrast with the extravagance of the Hopper monument, there are several small rustic eighteenth-century gravestones, movingly carved by local masons, which hardly rise above the long grass.*

EIGHTEENTH-CENTURY CHURCHES AS PARKLAND ORNAMENTS: AN INTRODUCTION

ST ANDREW, GUNTON, NORFOLK

ALL SAINTS, NUNEHAM COURTENAY, OXFORDSHIRE

ST MARY MAGDALENE, CROOME D'ABITOT, WORCESTERSHIRE

AT THE BEGINNING OF THE EIGHTEENTH CENTURY the aristocracy and landed gentry were provided with a new impetus for the building of large country houses in great numbers all over England. The impetus was twofold. The rejection of Gothic architecture and the return to the Classical architecture of ancient Rome, which had occurred in fifteenth century Italy, had in only a limited and piecemeal way in the sixteenth and seventeenth centuries reached England, where the majority had, for geographical, religious and political reasons, remained conservatively attached to the traditional. However, the years around 1700 saw the scholarly and wealthy sections of English society embrace the new architecture as their contact with mainland Europe increased. This provided the first impetus: to replace older medieval houses and castles which now seemed very old-fashioned with the Classical buildings of a new enlightenment. The second impetus was provided by the emergence of new ideas as to how a great country house should relate to the land immediately surrounding it.

Whatever grand houses the aristocracy may have kept in London, their real homes were in the country where they were landowners on a vast scale. The building of a new house was therefore nearly always accompanied by the laying out of a surrounding park in a new naturalistic way that was to become characteristically English, very different from the formality of previous times. The name of Lancelot 'Capability' Brown (1716–83) is associated more than any other with the creation of these parks, as he designed and worked on hundreds of properties over a period of fifty years. Initially the very private domain of the rich and the guests they wished to impress, these stately homes and their parks are now enjoyed by the

English public and foreign visitors in their millions every year. Typically, one enters through elegant wrought-iron gates between majestic gateposts with lodges on either side. A curving driveway leads across expanses of grassland with large trees growing singly or in groups with more extensive woods on a low hill in the distance. The surrounding land will rise and fall a little and shortly a serpentine lake will come into view fed by a small river. A handsome stone bridge may take the driveway across the lake and it is at this point that some artfully contrived curve will bring the great house itself into view. It is often in the style of Andrea Palladio (1508–80), a Venetian architect and prolific writer, whose ideas and work were at this time immensely popular in England, where its cool, calm nobility reflected the national mood and taste. The plan was often a symmetrical central block with a giant portico linked to two wings, left and right. These houses succeeded in conveying a sense of wealth and authority without excessive showiness. Such 'Palladian' houses sprang up in their hundreds in then English countryside, designed by the leading architects of the day. Today, the whole ensemble looks like the epitome of naturalness as though the house had been gently inserted into a pre-existing landscape. In fact, every feature was carefully contrived by its designer and an army of workmen: the trees, the undulation of the land, the lake and the river. These parks are not just an exercise in horticulture, they are one of the great English contributions to European art – the art of the Picturesque.

The introduction of architectural features into a park was important from the start. These could be minor features such as fountains, statues, obelisks and the like, but generally more substantial structures were desirable, ones that could be seen from the principal rooms of the house or from carefully selected viewpoints on walks in the park. As eyecatchers, such features would add an element of surprise and drama to the scene. Sometimes there was a readymade feature in the form of a medieval ruin. A particularly fortunate landowner might be able to incorporate the ruin of a great abbey into his park. In North Yorkshire, the home of several remote Cistercian monasteries, the owner of Studley Royal used the ruins of Fountains Abbey in this way, while at Dunscombe House near Helmsley the equally magnificent ruins of Rievaulx Abbey were made to be seen from a grass terrace high above them. If genuine ruins were not available they could be manufactured: abbeys, castles and all kinds of 'follies'. If the owner wanted something more in tune with the architecture of the house he would turn to ancient Rome or Greece for the erection of a small replica temple – rectangular, circular or in the form of a Greek cross with a handsome portico facing the viewer. Some parks, such as those at Stowe in Buckinghamshire, Rousham in Oxfordshire and Stourhead in Wiltshire, were provided with numerous features of this type.

There was another sort of 'temple' that could be used as an eyecatcher. A number of landowners hit upon the idea of demolishing an ancient parish church which was in the neighbouring village, or perhaps within the park itself, and creating in its place a 'temple church' in the new Palladian style, strategically placed so that it could be seen from the house. This had little to do with piety or the spiritual needs of the family or the local people. It was simply a form of aggrandisement to adorn the view. The idea seems extraordinary today: a new parish church, isolated from the village it served, with no regard for its people's convenience. But this was a time when a noble family reigned supreme in its locality. For those attending services today in this type of parish church the same inconvenience must still apply, albeit lessened by the use of motor transport. Inevitably, however, a large number of these churches have passed to the care of the Trust. Inconvenience, falling congregations and the reluctance of landed families to provide the support that they gave in the past, as many left their ancestral homes, led to redundancy. Visitors

Lancelot 'Capability' Brown (1716–83). He laid out the grounds at Nuneham Courtenay, Oxfordshire, and Croome d'Abitot, Worcestershire, where the churches were built as parkland ornaments. Painting by Nathaniel Dance.

to these churches deep within the walls of parks have a three-for-the-price-of-one experience in catching sight of a great house (not necessarily open to the public), and a beautiful park in addition to the church. The latter was invariably built to a liberal budget by the leading architects of the day and, as they have been largely in the control of the family as opposed to the clergy, they have nearly all escaped Victorian restorations to retain their original high-quality furnishings. It is often not easy to find parkland churches; many visitors to an area may not even be aware of their existence as it may be impossible to advertise their presence at a park entrance. Consequently, many will feel hesitant to enter private property, but there is always a public right of way to a parish church and its churchyard. The grounds as a whole, however, are generally private. The Trust's county guide leaflets and website will provide information.

21. ST ANDREW, GUNTON, NORFOLK

ARCHITECTURAL ORNAMENT IN A STATELY PARK (1): THE ROMAN TEMPLE

GUNTON IS ABOUT FIVE MILES inland from Cromer on the north-east Norfolk coast. The county shows two faces: one of busy seaside towns and villages popular with holidaymakers and one of a secretive rural interior largely unknown to visitors but loved by those who enjoy ancient churches. Gunton belongs very much to the latter. It has never been a populous parish since it has always been associated with a large house and park rather than a traditional village. The two buildings that are the subject of this chapter belong to the middle of the eighteenth century when the population of the parish was about a hundred. Today it is less than fifty. The Gunton estate has Saxon origins.

After belonging to bishops and passing through several families it came in 1639 to the Harbord family, who served at the courts of Charles I and II. Their descendants have lived at Gunton ever since.

The parish church, like the community it served, has always been centred on the estate, and the present building lies within the park, one of the larger of its kind. One enters through tall gates with adjacent lodges. The driveway passes first through a wooded area and then close to a lake, then runs directly in front of Gunton Hall. A Jacobean house which the Harbords inherited was rebuilt for them by Matthew Brettingham in the mid-1740s and extended by James Wyatt in 1785.

LEFT *The portico of the church built by Robert Adam in 1769 faces the house. It is typical of many town and city churches of the time and its presence inside a wood inside a park in the heart of rural Norfolk always surprises.*

RIGHT *Gunton Hall, as seen from the driveway to the church through the park. This section, built in 1785, is only part of the original house. The main entrance front faces the church hidden in the wood in the right.*

The effect of the interior is dominated by the contrast between the dark woodwork and the white plasterwork. This view from the chancel shows the west gallery and organ. The seating originally faced across the aisle collegiate style.

a wood within a park deep in rural Norfolk it is an extraordinary sight, the more so because it is encountered so unexpectedly.

The historical background to the creation of this type of church has been described on pages 102–3. Sir William Harbord, later first Baron Suffield, wanted a church which would be a prominent eyecatcher seen from the main rooms of the Hall. In 1766 he obtained a faculty from the Bishop of Norwich for the demolition of the medieval parish church and in 1769 commissioned the eminent Neoclassical architect Robert Adam to design the new church in a style that would match the Hall. The choice of architect tells something about the wealth of the family. Adam's church followed the plan and elevation of a Roman temple in its essentials. The pro-style portico has four Tuscan Doric columns with an architrave and pediment above with just a little restrained paterae decoration. It is a dignified and noble structure, which from the start was intended to be seen as a garden temple partly hidden within a glade. Thus there is no paved forecourt: grass extends right to the steps of the building. In wet weather it is no place for smart Sunday morning shoes.

The church is entered through a tall doorway with plain moldings. This leads into a circular vestibule with stairs rising to a gallery. The interior beyond is a simple rectangle. Robert Adam is famous more for the interior planning and decoration of town and country houses than as a church builder. In the former he created the grandest effects: majestic entrance halls with splendid staircases; salons, libraries and dining rooms of ingenious plan with apses and alcoves separated from the main room by Classical columns. But above all else he is associated with ravishingly beautiful plasterwork with mouldings adorning his walls and ceilings, work of exquisite delicacy based on ancient Greek, Etruscan and Roman motifs. In Gunton church he opted for more restrained effects. The overall impact is the

Much of Brettingham's building was gutted by fire in 1882 and never reconstructed, but Wyatt's extension still makes a substantial mansion. It is of light grey brick with central pediments on the two principal fronts. A little way beyond the Hall vehicles must park where the drive gives way to a path leading into a wood, and then a small clearing where the east front of the Hall is just visible between the trees. In the centre of the clearing facing the Hall is the giant Classical temple-style portico of the parish church of St Andrew. This would be a handsome if unremarkable building on the high street of a market town or in a square in the Georgian quarter of a large city, but here in contrast between dark and bright areas of colour. The floor is made up of the black and white marble tiles beloved by the eighteenth century in grand rooms. Almost everything above ground level is either dark brown woodwork or gleaming white plasterwork on walls and ceiling. The wooden west gallery has a front of three bays divided by fluted Ionic pilasters whose gilded capitals and their counterparts at the east end are the only minor pieces of ostentation in sight. To the left and right of the central doorway there are raised stalls for the family. The tall organ in the gallery above is nineteenth century, its wood matching the gallery front. In the body of the church the seating was originally collegiate style, facing inwards on either side of the centre aisle. It was rearranged to face the chancel after the First World War. A plaster frieze runs around the walls below the windows. A pretty cornice divides off the ceiling, which has a beautiful central circlet of feathers and foliage. The delicacy of the plasterwork is typical of Adam but understandably more understated than the lively intricacy and colour of his domestic interiors.

The chancel is defined only by curved steps raising it above the nave. The east wall is panelled in the same dark wood as elsewhere with fluted columns either side of the altar. Their gilded capitals echo those of the west gallery. Behind the altar is a copy of a sixteenth-century Florentine painting of the Virgin Mary with the infant Christ and her cousin Elizabeth with her son John the Baptist. It was presented by Lady Suffield in the early twentieth century.

Strangely in a church which one would have expected to have served as a family mausoleum, there are no large monuments, despite the wealth of the family. A portrait medallion of Lady Suffield (d. 1911) is almost alone.

Secrecy and silence are characteristics of Trust churches. In this place they seem to have a strangely eerie quality. The interior is decidedly sombre and the complete absence of any sign of

present activity makes the presence of the past more tangible. The closing of the heavy oak door creates a hollow echo within the portico and the encircling wood. A sense of abandonment makes this one of the ghostliest of redundant churches.

A parish of less than one hundred people can never have been viable, dependent always on the patronage of a single family. As long ago as 1757 the 'livings' of Gunton and neighbouring Hanworth were united, a very early example of this sort of action. It was not until 1976 that the two parishes were united. St Andrew's was declared redundant in the following year and passed into the care of the Trust.

The altar in front of the panelled east wall. The picture of the Virgin Mary and St Elizabeth with the infant Christ and John the Baptist is a copy of a sixteenth-century Florentine work.

22. ALL SAINTS, NUNEHAM COURTENAY, OXFORDSHIRE

ARCHITECTURAL ORNAMENT IN A STATELY PARK (II):
THE CHURCH OF A BANISHED VILLAGE

Nuneham Courtenay is a village about 7 miles south-east of Oxford on the busy Dorchester road where there is a line of cottages on either side. Their uniformity in an eighteenth-century style clearly indicates that they were planted here by command and although they are neatly ordered in the Classical way they are not as attractive as a village that has evolved naturally. An inconspicuous opening leads into a lane between fields, which shortly passes a small late-nineteenth-century church. It is not for another mile or so that the signs of fine parkland become apparent. From a spacious car park it is only a short walk to a spot where you can look down across expansive lawns to a mansion built of local 'ironstone', a limestone stained deep brown by oxides of iron.

The story of the buildings described here begins when the estate was bought in 1710 by Sir Simon Harcourt, who at the same time retained the family property at Stanton Harcourt about 10 miles away to the west of Oxford. The heads of the family became successively barons, viscounts and earls. The 1st Earl Harcourt celebrated his elevation by demolishing the medieval manor house and replacing it on the same site with the present mansion in the 1750s. He and his successors recognised the picturesque landscaping potential of the extensive grounds. In order to realise that potential it was deemed necessary to get rid of the village and its parish church, which had always stood close to the old manor house in the medieval way. The Earl's decision is said to have been the inspiration for Oliver Goldsmith's poem 'Deserted Village'.

The man of wealth and pride;
Takes up a space that many poor supply'd
Space for his lake, his park's extended bounds
Space for his horses, equipage and hounds.

The grounds as they were eventually created were described by Horace Walpole in 1780 as 'the most beautiful in the world'. 'Capability' Brown (pages 102–3) was closely involved in the

OPPOSITE *The new church was built as an eyecatching ornament by the 1st Earl Harcourt in 1764. The grand portico is a deception, a fake entrance designed to face the house which lies to the right of this view.*

LEFT *The main entrance front of Nuneham Courtenay House, which was first built in 1756 and subsequently much extended. The medieval village and parish church lay immediately to the right of the house before they were demolished. The village was banished outside the park and the church was rebuilt on rising ground a few hundred yards away, beyond the right-hand edge of the photograph.*

landscaping. The destruction of the old village accounts for the subsequent construction of the brick cottages on the main road. (The villagers were lucky by eighteenth-century standards. They were given not only cottages but a garden each to compensate for the lack of a village green. Similar lordly action in other places left the evicted people to fend for themselves.)

It was now the fashion for those planning parks around family seats to erect major architectural ornaments, as described on pages 102–3. The demolition of the medieval church would have been allowed on the condition that the earl provide a new one. Instead of erecting it on the main road where it would have been convenient for the villagers, the Earl planned the new church as an eyecatcher prominently placed on rising ground in full view of the house a few hundred yards away. The design is partly his own, partly that of James Stuart, an architect who was one of the early advocates of a Classical architecture based on ancient Greek rather than Roman precedents. The fact that the position of the new church involved a walk of about 2 miles from the nearest of the village cottages would have been the least of the Earl's concerns. The church was completed in 1764. The view of the building shown here is rather misleading. The giant portico is not a real entrance, only a showpiece front to be seen from the house, which lies to the right. The columns lead only to a blank wall; the real entrance is on an adjacecent side.

The interior produces other surprises. From the outside the dome suggests a central plan. The view from the entrance shows that it is narrowly longnitudinal, although it does not show the two pairs of transepts. The bare white-plastered walls, ceiling and dome have a 'bleak and spartan' appearance in a Neoclassical way. It is immediately noticed how they contrast sharply with the almost black wooden furniture. The latter is not original. In 1872 the then head of the family built yet another 'new' church close to the village, probably at the request of the rector and leading villagers. This is the church seen on the way into the park (above). Thus the 1st Earl's church, the original 'new' church now became the 'old' church. That title is often used today. The church in the park then became essentially a house chapel serving the family. Whatever seating was provided originally, and it could not have been extensive, was replaced by a limited number of stalls facing each other across the nave. One set was placed near the chancel and oddly, another set near the entrance. They are Baroque pieces of work brought from Italy, as is the font cover in the transept, which serves as a baptistery.

ABOVE *The real entrance to the church is a semi-circular portico at the west end of the church.*

RIGHT *The narrowly longitudinal interior seen from the entrance. The white walls and dome and the severely plain architecture contrast with the dark wood of the ornate Baroque furnishings inserted in the late nineteenth century.*

The church has numerous Harcourt monuments and some busts made from life. Most of them were inserted after the villagers moved out. Their white marble adds to the whiteness of the structure. Julian Harcourt, who died in 1862 aged two years, is shown on his deathbed, a typical piece of Victorian sentiment at a time when infant deaths were commonplace. William Harcourt, who died in 1831, is shown seated. The north transept has several monuments. The most prominent is that of Sir William George Harcourt M.P. (d. 1904), who served as Chancellor of the Exchequer and Leader of the House of Commons. The austerely plain architecture behind can be noticed. Funeral hatchments on the walls span the whole of the nineteenth century.

The wealth and power of the eighteenth-century English aristocracy is amply demonstrated at Nuneham Courtenay in the creation of the house and park, the destruction and translation of an entire village and the destruction and rebuilding of a parish church to suit the vanity of an earl. Most empires, including family empires, dissolve away. During the Second World War, when the grounds became an army camp, they were

despoiled and neglected for years afterwards. The Harcourt family abandoned Nuneham Courtenay in 1948 and returned to Stanton Harcourt, After that the parkland church ceased to be even a family chapel and fell into disrepair. The estate was sold to Oxford University, who in turn leased it to other organisations. To add irony to the sad story, the Harcourts' new church built in 1872 was itself declared redundant some years ago. It is now a geological store for Oxford University.

The future looks brighter. The house and park are currently occupied by the Brahma Kumaris World Spirituality Movement, which provides day and residential courses to bring Eastern culture to the West. It maintains the house and and partly restored grounds in impeccable condition. The reception desk in the house holds the key for the nearby church, which passed into the care of the Trust in 1980 so that its future also is secure.

JVLIAN
ELDEST SON OF
WILLIAM AND THÉRÈSE

ABOVE LEFT *The Baroque font cover in the baptistery is another of the late-nineteenth-century insertions.*

ABOVE RIGHT *The monument to Julian Harcourt, who died in 1862 aged two years, shows him on his deathbed. Sentimental displays of grief were usual at a time when infant deaths were commonplace.*

BELOW LEFT *Statue of Willaim Harcourt, who died in 1831.*

BELOW RIGHT *The north transept has several family monuments. The largest is the prostrate effigy of Sir William George Harcourt M.P., Chancellor of the Exchequer and Leader of the House of Commons, who died in 1904.*

23. ST MARY MAGDALENE, CROOME D'ABITOT, WORCESTERSHIRE

ARCHITECTURAL ORNAMENT IN A STATELY PARK (III): THE GOTHICK FANTASY

LEFT *Croome Court was built in 1751 in the Palladian style by 'Capability' Brown, who was here involved as much in the architecture as the landscape.*

ABOVE *The grand entrance to Croome Park. The electronically operated gates are a modern touch. The church is a few hundred yards to the right.*

CROOME D'ABITOT HAS ALWAYS BEEN an estate rather than a village or parish. It lies about 7 miles due east of the Malvern Hills and since the intervening land is fairly flat there is a splendid view of the high ridge running north–south like a sharply creased piece of paper standing on its edges. The man-made line of the M5 motorway snakes along the western edge of the park without doing too much damage to its peace and seclusion. Such rural highways with limited access points can sometimes protect the surrounding countryside. The unusual name of the estate is linked with the villages of Earls Croome and Hill Croome a few miles to the south, each of which lies close to a winding stream (*crombe* in Old English). In 1165, Robert d'Abitot, from St Jean d'Abbetot in Normandy, bought land here and the family gradually extended their holding. The village and manor had their own church by the thirteenth century, but it was a chapelry of Ripple 5 miles to the south. In 1592 the manor was sold to Thomas Coventry. His son, also Thomas, was made Lord Keeper of the Great Seal and was created Baron Coventry in 1628. The latter's grandson became 1st Earl of Coventry in 1697. Over the generations the family became rich through their involvement in politics and law. The 6th Earl, who succeeded in 1751 at the age of thirty, had great ambitions for developing the estate. A late-seventeenth-

century house was no longer at the height of fashion and much of the estate was a swampy morass as it lay within the confluence area of the Rivers Severn and Avon, which flooded frequently. 'Capability' Brown, now rising to fame, was called in to lay out new grounds. In the event his involvement with Croome was to be much greater. The Earl demolished the old house and asked Brown to design a fashionable Palladian building to replace it. Although primarily a landscaper, Brown had worked alongside the most distinguished architects of the period and during his career designed several houses within his own landscapes. A grand entrance to the park leads downwards to the house, which is typically Palladian in its cool nobility. The stone is local buff limestone. The work required the draining of the land beneath and a start on more extensive drainage in the park.

In 1758, the Earl obtained a faculty from the Bishop of Worcester for demolishing the old church alongside the new house on the grounds that it was derelict and inconveniently

placed for the parishioners. In reality, it was inconveniently placed for the Earl in the laying out of the planned park. Furthermore, he wished to copy the example of several of his contemporaries and erect a new church as an eyecatcher in the park. The land immediately in front of the house was fairly flat, but on one side it rose quite steeply to a long ridge. This provided an ideal site for the proposed church, near enough to be clearly seen outlined on the skyline, sufficiently distant not to dominate the house or intrude upon its privacy. At first the plan was for a Classical building, as at Gunton and Nuneham Courtenay, but the idea changed to adopt what was then a novel

strand in English architectural history. We have seen that the eighteenth century was a period committed to Classical architecture. However, the monuments of medieval Gothic architecture were all around in the form of palaces, castles, cathedrals and most of all in thousands of parish churches in cities, towns and villages. Nor had the practice of Gothic architecture ever become entirely extinct. Eminent seventeenth- and eighteenth-century architects could work in the old style when the situation or client demanded. Inspired by medieval buildings and idealised versions of medieval life, a number of the aristocracy and gentry developed a romantic

Seen from the house, the new church of 1763 perched on a ridge is a perfect parkland eyecatcher.

LEFT *A close-up view of the church. It is more convincingly medieval than many imitation 'Gothick' churches of its date.*

ABOVE *The porch and west door within the tower. The proportions and details are eighteenth-century Gothick, not medieval.*

attachment to the idea of a 'Merrie England' of the Middle Ages, and in building that meant Gothic. The form of Gothic these men created had few of the true structural elements of the original. It was a fanciful, romantic version in which Gothic ornament was superficially attached to wall and roof surfaces, known today as 'Gothick'. The serious Gothic Revival, based on real medieval precedents did not emerge until the 1830s.

Work on the new church began in 1763. The exterior is attributed to Brown and the interior to Robert Adam, who was then designing the interiors of the house. The building is one of the more serious examples of early Gothic and looks convincingly medieval on its ridgetop site when seen from the house. From this viewpoint it fits perfectly the description of the satirist Charles Churchill (1732–64), who had seen several of its kind:

> Temples which, built aloft in air
> May serve for show, if not for prayer

The church consists of chancel, nave with aisles and west tower. The stone is the same as the house. Entry is through a porch, which forms the ground stage of the tower. Seen close up the details betray its date in its height, roof vault and

LEFT *The interior, 'of the highest merit', was created by Robert Adam. Seen from the chancel, the nave has slender columns supporting a decorated plaster roof, all a delicate Georgian version of medieval Gothic.*

ABOVE *The wooden font, 'exquisite in shape and exquisite in detail'.*

tall double doors which are clearly Gothick. The windows higher up and the battlements are more convincingly medieval.

The interior is 'of the highest merit', as one would expect from an interior designer of Adam's standing. Here we are back to Georgian Gothick, with slender piers supporting a coved roof with pretty stucco decoration. However, the chancel is long in the medieval way. Usually the eighteenth century favoured short chancels as it placed little emphasis on the altar and celebration of the eucharist. The wooden font at the west end is 'exquisite in shape and exquisite in detail'.

The long chancel provides an excellent setting for the Coventry family monuments, which face each other on either side. They were all made for the old church at the time when the heads of the family were barons before the creation of the earldom. Their translation to the new church was made a condition for the demolition of the old. The use of a combination of black and white Italian marbles in monuments was popular throughout the seventeenth century. In the bright light from the large clear glass windows the effect is particularly striking. The 1st Lord Coventry (d. 1639) reclines beneath a tall arch. As Lord Keeper of the Great Seal, his mace of office lies in front of him. An allegorical figure of Justice holds the seal with a portrait of Charles I. The 2nd Lord (d. 1661) lies rather awkwardly beneath a square structure supported by twisted columns. The monument to his wife shows her holding a baby, the way of indicating a death in childbirth, while two sons kneel at her feet. The 4th Lord (d. 1687) reclines on a sarcophagus reaching out to an allegorical figure of Faith, who originally held a crown to bestow upon him. The monument is by Grinling Gibbons, who worked in stone as well as wood. The garlands at the top of the monument 'are worthy of him'.

As they leave, visitors have a particularly good view across to the west from the elevated position outside the tower: dramatic nature in the distant Malvern Hills, gentle farmland in the mid-distance, idyllic man-made parkland below and one of the most beautiful and interesting of eighteenth-century churches in England behind. All that is combined with perfect stillness and silence. It is what visitors to Trust churches come to expect.

In the years after the Second World War, the story at Croome was very similar to that at Nuneham Courtenay. The family left Croome in 1949 and the house became first a school, then a hotel, before being sold to another family. During this time the grounds became an overgrown wilderness and the numerous ornamental buildings became dilapidated. Despite the efforts of a small group of parishioners to keep the church going, its maintenance in the absence of the family became impossible. But, as at Nuneham Courtenay, recovery followed. The property was repossessed by a Coventry family trust and leased to the National Trust, which is engaged in a long-term project to restore the grounds to Brown's vision. Since 1975, the church has been cared for by the Trust.

The seventeenth-century monuments of the Coventry family in the chancel are all in a striking combination of black and white Italian marbles.

ABOVE LEFT *The 1st Lord Coventry (d. 1639) reclines under an arch reaching up to the ceiling. He was Lord Keeper of the Great Seal of England under Charles I.*

LEFT *On one side of the monument a female figure of Justice holds the Great Seal imprinted with a likeness of Charles I.*

TOP *The 2nd Lord Coventry (d. 1661) lies awkwardly beneath a structure with twisted columns.*

ABOVE *The wife of the 2nd Lord (d. 1634). Left: she holds a baby, indicating her death in childbirth; right: two of her sons kneel at her feet.*

RIGHT *The 4th Lord (d. 1687) reclines reaching out in supplication to a figure of Faith. The sculptor was Grinling Gibbons, which tells something of the family's wealth.*

24. ST MARY MAGDALENE, STAPLEFORD, LEICESTERSHIRE

ARCHITECTURAL INNOVATION FOR A CLERGYMAN–EARL

STAPLEFORD IS A SCATTERED PARISH in quiet countryside a few miles south-east of Melton Mowbray. There have been manor houses and greater houses here since the Norman Conquest which were initially owned by the Crown and its nominees. The estate came to Robert Sherard in 1402 and remained in the family for the next 500 years. Thomas Sherard built a substantial manor house in c.1500, a little of which remains. William Sherard was knighted by James I and made Baron Leitrim by Charles I. He greatly enlarged the house in the 1630s in an ornate Jacobean Gothic style that forms a substantial part of the present Hall. The 2nd Baron, Bennet Sherard, added new wings in the 1670s in a restrained Classical style.

His son, also Bennet (1677–1732) was created Baron Harborough in 1714 (Market Harborough is about 20 miles to the south), a viscount in 1715 and 1st Earl of Harborough in 1719 – a rapid advance by any standards. The 4th Earl, Robert (1719–99), had not expected to succeed his brother and was rector of nearby Teigh. This clergyman-earl continued the tradition of improving the estate. In the 1780s he demolished the medieval parish church, which stood about 200 yards from the Hall, and replaced it on the same site with a new building. This was never intended to be used as an eyecatcher in the park, as was the case at Gunton, Nuneham Courtenay and Croome d'Abitot previously. Perhaps as a clergyman the Earl had too much respect for this church and the Church generally. The grounds were laid out by 'Capability' Brown at the same time.

They are now entered from a single-track road with passing places, which gives some indication of the quietness of the place. Normally on entering such a park visitors are taken to the house on a curving driveway that sweeps through an expansive vista of grassland scattered with trees and various ornamental features positioned for maximum picturesque effect. At Stapleford one immediately enters dense woodland with a network of intersecting driveways darkened by the leafy canopy overhead. Almost at once the white stone church set back from the driveway is enticingly half-visible among the trees that surround the spacious churchyard. The driveways lead away to the Hall beyond. At the time that the church was built, the Earl had the adjacent village moved away outside the park, as

BELOW *The elegant Classical east front of the newer part of Stapleford Hall was built in the 1670s by Bennet Sherard, Baron Leitrim. His son became the 1st Earl of Harborough.*

OPPOSITE *The church of St Mary Magdalene is hidden away in a wooded corner of the grounds of the Hall, which is a few hundred yards away.*

The church was built in 1783 by the 4th Earl of Harborough to replace a medieval church on the same site. It is a remarkably early example of an authentic Gothic Revival church, a style that did not become widespread until fifty years later.

at Nuneham Courtenay and Croome d'Abitot. What remains now is a church of total seclusion and peace, where the outside world seems completely cut off.

The Earl employed George Richardson as his architect. He was a draughtsman in the London office of Robert Adam, whose work we have also seen at Gunton and Croome. Richardson's design for the church was considered to be sufficiently distinguished to be exhibited at the

Royal Academy in 1783. The eighteenth century was a period mainly committed to Classical architecture in one form or another. However, Croome d'Abitot church demonstrated how a number of aristocratic patrons developed a taste for a romantic, decorative style of 'Gothick' architecture. The serious Gothic Revival based on genuine medieval precedents did not emerge until the 1830s. 'Capability' Brown's design for the exterior of Croome went some way towards

ABOVE *Above the west entrance of the tower are the arms of the Sherard family, Earls of Harborough.*

ABOVE RIGHT *The arms of families connected with the Sherards adorn the walls of the nave.*

RIGHT *The porch beneath the tower has a pretty plaster ceiling with gilded angels.*

medieval realism; Robert Adam's interior much less so. Richardson's design for Stapleford made a further effort. It is 'outstanding in the Gothic field for its date . . . the Gothic handled with remarkable restraint and without fancies'. The church consists of a wide aisleless nave, chancel, shallowly projecting transepts and west tower. It was built of the same unusually white limestone that was used in the Hall a hundred years earlier. Most of the English limestones are stained anything from pale cream through buff to brown due to the presence of oxides of iron. The Stapleford stone resembles Portland limestone from the Dorset coast in its lack of colour, the latter made popular for building by Christopher Wren in the seventeenth century. St Mary Magdalene looks as though it was one of his City of London churches transplanted here. The nave and tower of the church are topped by pretty balustrading. Over the west door is an

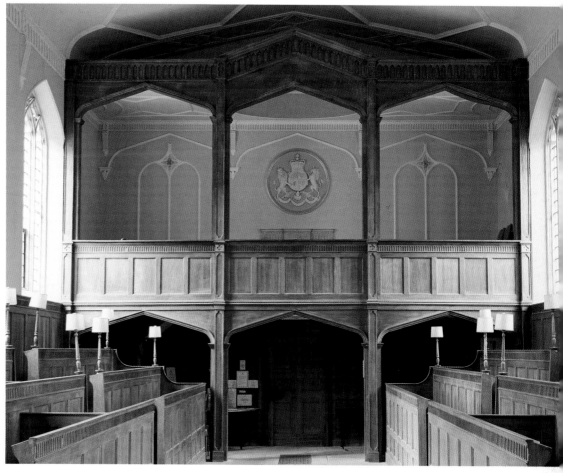

LEFT *The spacious nave has pews arranged collegiate style facing each other across the central aisle.*

ABOVE *The family pew of the earls is a gallery at the west end.*

ogee hood mould and the arms of the Sherards. Around the sides there are the arms of various families connected with the Sherards, a typical display of aristocratic pride in ancestry.

The door leads into a vestibule forming the ground floor of the tower. It has a pretty plaster vault with gilded angels at the centre and a handsome version of the Trust's plaque The interior beyond is flooded with light from the large clear glass windows. (The eighteenth-century taste for Gothic seldom extended to large areas of stained glass.) The layout of the nave is not unusual for the time, although it would never have been seen in a medieval parish church. On either side of the wide central aisle the benches face other other in the style of Oxbridge colleges, with which the 4th Earl would have been familiar. The family had their own seating in the west gallery, where they would not have to mix with their servants or village people.

It has a pretty fireplace where a fire would no doubt have been lit well in advance of Sunday service by a servant. Above it are the Royal Arms of George III cast in plaster.

There are, as expected, many fine monuments to the Sherards, most of them brought from the old church. The two transepts were designed to take them, so that although they are large they do not intrude upon the general space of the church or distract at services. Perhaps we see in this the mind of an earl who was also a clergyman. The oldest monument is to the first Baron Leitrim (above), who died in 1640, and his wife. It is a sumptuous monument of black and white marbles 'fully good enough to be in Westminster Abbey'. The effigies in beautifully carved dresses lie on a tomb chest surrounded by minature figures of their eight kneeling children. Above and behind this in the south transept within a Gothic arch are several busts of Sherards who died between 1699 and 1799, including that of Robert the 4th Earl who built the church. The massive monument to the 1st Earl (d. 1732) faces them in the

north transept. It was carved by John Michael Rysbrack (1694–1770), one of the greatest sculptors of the eighteenth century, whose works appear in Westminster Abbey. It shows the Earl dressed in Roman costume half-reclining next to his countess and an infant child, 'a beautifully composed group'. Behind the figures a grey marble obelisk reaches up to the ceiling. At the top are portrait medallions of the Earl and Countess and a family shield.

Its pioneering architecture, furnishings and monuments give Stapleford a significant place in English architectural history. It is typical of English churches that architecture and art of this quality should be hidden away in a place where it is possible to stay several hours without seeing another soul.

The 6th Earl died in 1859 without issue. The Hall passed by sale to two other families before becoming a country house hotel in 1987. The grounds are private but there is a public right of way to the churh which is open daily. It was vested in the Trust in 1996.

FAR LEFT *The family pew is fitted with a fireplace to be lit by a servant on Sunday mornings in winter. The Royal Arms of George III are cast in plaster above.*

LEFT *High up on the wall of the south transept are busts of the barons and earls who died between 1699 and 1799.*

RIGHT *Monument to Robert Sherard, 1st Baron Leitrim (d. 1640) and his wife. Miniatures of their children surround the effigies. The sumptuous carving of figures and dresses is 'fully good enough for Westminster Abbey'.*

RIGHT BELOW *A section of the finely composed and sculpted family monument of the 1st Earl of Harborough (d. 1732). He is shown in Roman dress with his wife and child. The work is by leading eighteenth-century sculptor John Michael Rysbrack.*

The east end of the church. Local slate prevails: stone blocks in the walls and tiles on the roofs. The gravestones are also slate.

25. ST PETROCK, PARRACOMBE, DEVON

A THEATRICAL INTERIOR ON THE EDGE OF EXMOOR

Parracombe is a village in the north-west corner of Exmoor about 3 miles inland from the Bristol Channel, nestling deep down in the narrow, steep-sided combe (valley) of the name. The original church dedicated to St Petrock (a seventh-century Cornish saint) is, however, high up at the top of the combe surrounded by a separate little group of houses. Towards the end of the nineteenth century the building was structurally unstable and in 1879 it was proposed to demolish the church and build anew on the same site. This suggestion was strongly opposed not only in the village but throughout the county and beyond. John Ruskin, the architectural historian and writer, led the protests and proposed that the old church be left and a new church be built down in the combe where most of the village had by then become established. It was clear that the old church, particularly its interior, which reflected the history of the village over several centuries, was greatly loved. As a result Christ Church was built in the centre of the village and extensive conservation work was carried out on

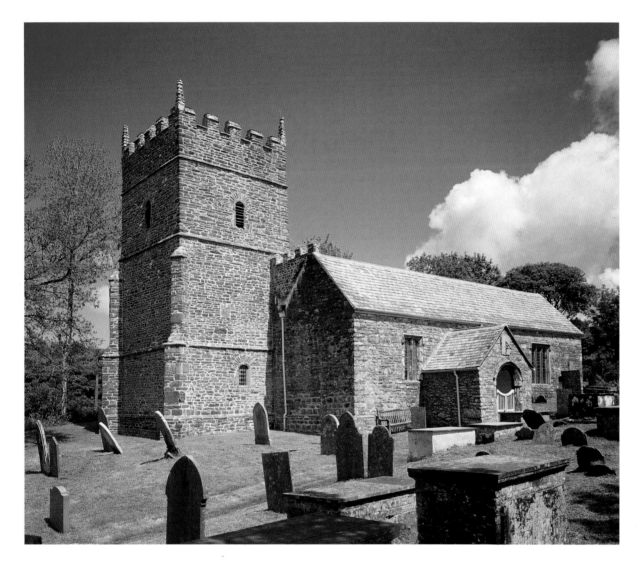

The low tower is in proportion to the squat body of the church behind. The lack of ornamental carvings on either reflects the hardness of slate.

St Petrock's, work that was continued at various periods throughout the twentieth century.

The church is surrounded by a large churchyard bordered by a few old cottages and the tors of Exmoor are visible from the gate. The church and its churchyard are an essay in slate, one of the many building stones in which Devon is rich. The roof is tiled in slate and the walls are roughly hewn block slate. Most of the gravestones too are slate, here smoothly cut. Slate is hard and therefore durable but it is not as easy to carve decoratively as many limestones and sandstones. As a result the church is a plain, rugged building with little ornament, which is not inappropriate in a moorland situation. It is also rather squat, a result of the West Country practice of building naves that were no higher than the aisles, without

a clerestory. The tower keeps the same low proportions. The earliest church may have been Norman but there is nothing now visible earlier than the thirteenth century. Most of the building with its straight-headed windows is late-fifteenth or early-sixteenth century.

Despite the lack of a clerestory the large clear-glass aisle windows flood the interior with light and the tall widely distanced piers give a sense of spaciousness. It is not, however, the architecture that one remembers principally but the untouched late medieval and eighteenth-century furnishings. Standing in the middle of the nave there is a sense of being in a theatre. Looking to the west the box pews and benches at the back are raked as in an auditorium. Looking to the east the chancel is separated from the nave by a screen which in its

lower parts is open medieval tracery. Above that a solid eighteenth-century tympanum is painted with the Hanoverian arms, the Ten Commandments, Apostles' Creed and Lord's Prayer. The whole structure makes the chancel look like a stage separated from the auditorium by a proscenium arch. On its south side is a three-decker pulpit. Within the chancel there is a complete Puritan or Low Church arrangement for the celebration of the eucharist (as at Pilling, page 93). A plain 'holy table' (the word 'altar' was reminiscent of popery at that time) is bordered by communion rails on three sides to prevent any suggestion that the minister officiating at the table was separate from the people in any special way. In the chancel there is a moving wall tablet commemorating an infant death and in the nave there are characteristic eighteenth-century wall texts.

The village and parish maintained two churches, old and new, until 1969, when St Petrock's was vested in the Trust. John Ruskin said that the demolition of St Petrock's would be an 'act of vandalism', and most modern visitors would agree.

ABOVE LEFT *The nave seen from the chancel. The eighteenth-century seating at the back is raked as in a theatre.*

ABOVE RIGHT *The altar is the original Puritan arrangement with a holy table surrounded by communion rails on three sides.*

RIGHT *An eighteenth-century wall text in the nave.*

RIGHT BELOW *Commemoration of an eighteenth-century infant death on a chancel wall.*

OPPOSITE *The chancel arch cuts off the chancel as the proscenium arch of a stage. The lower part is medieval; the upper eighteenth-century tympanum has the Hanoverian Royal Arms and the traditional commandments and prayer boards.*

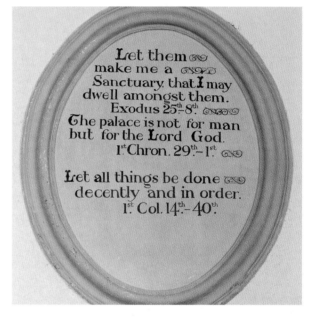

Let them make me a Sanctuary, that I may dwell amongst them. Exodus 25th.-8th.
The palace is not for man but for the Lord God. 1st Chron. 29th.-1st
Let all things be done decently and in order. 1st Col. 14th.-40th.

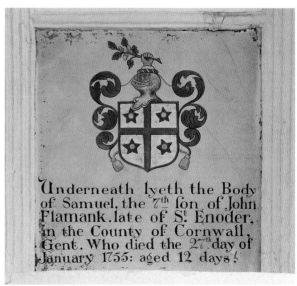

Underneath lyeth the Body of Samuel, the 7th son of John Flamank, late of St. Enoder, in the County of Cornwall, Gent. Who died the 27th day of January 1755: aged 12 days.

26. ST MARY, LEAD, NORTH YORKSHIRE

THE FORLORN CHAPEL OF A MEDIEVAL MANOR HOUSE

LEAD IS A RURAL AREA about 10 miles north-east of Leeds on one of the roads to Tadcaster. The name is derived from the Old English *hleodh*, which means a wood with a shelter. The Pennine hills have given way here to the gently rippling landscape of the Vale of York and the Pennine buildings have changed from the gritty buff sandstone blackened by centuries of smoke to the near-white of the band of magnesian limestone that runs down the Vale from north to south. The stone was quarried at Tadcaster from the early Middle Ages for use in buildings ranging in size from York Minster to Lead Chapel. Modern large-scale maps show only a Lead Mill Farm and a Lead Hall Farm without a village. John Leland (1506–52), the Tudor antiquarian and traveller, refers to 'Leade, a hamlet where Skargil had a fair manor place of tymber'. The latter was probably on the site of the present Lead Hall Farm. The sight of a tiny church measuring about 18 feet long and 12 feet wide standing rather

Without its manor house and village, the tiny fourteenth-century chapel stands forlornly alone in a field. The former manor house was beyond the trees, left.

A closer view of the chapel. It is built of local white magnesian limestone.

forlornly alone in a large field without a churchyard or any surrounding wall inevitably arouses curiosity and the urge to inspect. The bumps and hollows in the field indicate that there ms once a small village close to the manor house and chapel, as would be expected in a medieval manorial community. It is probable that that St Mary's was the private chapel of the manor house, not a parish church. The area was in the parish of Ryther until 1912, when it was transferred to Saxton, both villages which have parochial Norman churches.

The building is a simple rectangular box which might be any age but the Decorated Gothic windows point to the early fourteenth century. Fifteenth-century documents refer to a chancel, and excavations outside the east end have revealed its foundations. It is not known when it was demolished. The furnishings have a homely rusticity. The primitive open-backed benches may be late medieval. The three-decker pulpit tucked away in the north-east corner is eighteenth century. The wall texts carved in wood are probably early nineteenth century

In the late sixteenth century the chapel was reported as being in 'utter

'ruyne and decay', possibly due to a change in religious allegiances at the manor house at the time of the Reformation. It was restored in the eighteenth century as the furnishings indicate, but by 1930 it was again ruinous. It was saved by the members of the Ramblers' Association, whose members use local footpaths and frequently go in. Hard times returned after the Second World War until it was delivered into the safe hands of the Trust in 1980.

ABOVE LEFT *The interior has the simplest of rustic furnishings. The open-backed benches may be late medieval.*

ABOVE RIGHT *The three-decker eighteenth-century pulpit is the simplest of woodwork. Note the raised medieval gravestones in the floor.*

RIGHT *Two of the early-nineteenth-century wall texts urge the people to Christian virtues.*

27. THE BLESSED VIRGIN MARY, OLD DILTON, WILTSHIRE

A HARMONY OF WARM LIMESTONE AND WOODWORK

An elevated view of the church from the adjacent railway embankment. Its homely charm is enhanced by the warm cream-coloured limestone.

THE HAMLET OF OLD DILTON lies on a minor road within a triangle of three main roads that join Westbury, Warminster and Frome. Its residents thus get the best of two worlds: the peace of the gentle Wiltshire countryside combined with easy access to three market towns. The church is an early example of redundancy, albeit gradually phased redundancy. The village thrived during the period of the medieval wool industry but declined from the seventeenth century onwards. The population slowly drifted to Dilton Marsha a few miles away, where a new church was built in 1844. After that services were held at Old Dilton only on a very occasional basis. In the twentieth century the Society for the Protection of Ancient Buildings, founded by William Morris, was concerned for the state of the church and carried out extensive repairs between 1933 and 1953. It remained in the care of the parish until 1973 when it was finally declared redundant.

The building is in the fifteenth century Perpendicular Gothic style although the details of the porch point to an earlier church.

An 'entertaining' variety of windows includes those from the seventeenth and eighteenth centuries. It is a small, homely church made particularly lovable by its warm, cream-coloured Jurassic limestone and the matching limestone roof tiles. It has a nave with a north aisle, chancel and a little bell-cote with spire at the west end. A good elevated view of the church can be obtained from the embankment of the railway that runs from Westbury to Salisbury.

Since the congregation was already in decline in the early nineteenth century and since a new church had been provided near by, the interior escaped a restoration of the type that was common elsewhere in the latter part of the Victorian period. The church retains a complete set of eighteenth-century pine furnishings which reflect the pattern of worship at a time when the emphasis was on preaching The Word. A three-decker pulpit is placed against the middle of the south wall, as we have seen at several places elsewhere and box pews are packed into every square foot of available space. The old pine has bleached to a mellow buff echoing the warmth of the stonework. There is a nave west gallery and on the north side of the chancel there is a second gallery. This was once used as the village schoolroom. The arms of George III are placed above the entrance to the chancel.

The church was handed over to the Trust in 1974.

ABOVE *The interior looking to the east. The pulpit in the middle of the south wall is the focus of attention from all the box pews crammed into every available space.*

BELOW *The box pews in the north aisle and the west gallery beyond. Notice the tilt of the arcade piers.*

28. ST BARTHOLOMEW, RICHARDS CASTLE, HEREFORDSHIRE

A HILLTOP CHURCH AND CASTLE OVERLOOKING A WHOLE COUNTY

A FEW MILES SOUTH OF LUDLOW the main road to Hereford by-passes a steep hill where a minor road leads up to its broad flat top. This is a remarkable place scenically and historically. To the south there is a view across the county to the Black Mountains on the Welsh borders and westwards far into Worcestershire. The hilltop is a microcosm of early English history. It is the site of the moated Richards Castle, the eponymous medieval village, and the medieval church of St Bartholomew, which is extraordinarily large for such a remote and inaccessible place. There is now only a handful of cottages up here; the modern village has understandably migrated to the bottom of the hill.

The Richard who originally built the castle was Richard Fitz Scrob, one of the Norman nobles at the court of Edward the Confessor. Edward was half Norman through his mother Emma and again through her a cousin of William the future Conqueror. Edward had several powerful Norman friends to whom he made grants of lands, greatly resented by the Saxon nobility. Richard's son held the castle after the Conquest, by which time it was vital for William to have a line of castles all along the Welsh border to defend the western edge of

The church started as a garrison chapel for the adjacent Norman castle, and was then enlarged over several centuries. On a hill in north Herefordshire, it gazes south over much of the county.

his new kingdom from hostile Celts. Richard's castle grew in size and importance during the thiteenth and fourteenth centuries but it had become ruinous by the sixteenth century. The castle today is not one of those tidy ruins sitting among carefully manicured lawns. A wooden bridge crosses the moat, beyond which parts of the building rise to a considerable height enveloped in trees and a tangle of shrubs.

The church has two round-headed Norman windows to show that it dates from the time of the castle. The original church, which would have been essentially a garrison chapel, was considerably enlarged in later centuries. In the late thirteenth century a south aisle was added, whose east window has Geometrical Decorated tracery and ball-flower ornament. In the early fourteenth century the chancel was lengthened by which time Decorated tracery had developed into its flowing or curvilinear form and there is an excellent example in the east window.

The detached bell tower is of a kind rare in England and even more unusually it lies to the east of the church some 17 feet from the end of the chancel. It is severely plain without any butressing or adornment. Like others on the Welsh borders it probably had a defensive role.

The spaciousness of the church is even more impressive inside. The walls are all 'scraped', i.e. the plaster or limewash has all been removed to reveal the bare rough-hewn stonework which gives the interior a rugged castle-like atmosphere. The nave and long chancel seem to disappear away into the distance. The capitals of of the piers have the same Decorated ball-flower as on the aisle windows. Apart from its size, the most memorable feature of the interior is the large number of late-seventeenth-century box pews, all uniform and neatly aligned on

either side of the nave and south aisle. The pew of the prominent Salwey family in the north transept is of the same date. Several of their funeral hatchments are hung around the church.

It is a strange sensation to stand alone in total silence on the chancel steps facing the massed ranks of all those empty box pews as the imagination sees them filled with eighteenth- and nineteenth-century worshippers dressed in the Sunday finery of their times. It is extraordinary that such large congregations numbering several hundred people would make their way up here on foot or horseback from the surrounding farms and cottages. The church passed to the Trust in 2001.

ABOVE *The late-seventeenth-century pew of the Salwey family is alone in the north transept.*

LEFT *One of the funeral hatchments of the Salwey family.*

29. ST CUTHBERT, HOLME LACY, HEREFORDSHIRE

FOUR CENTURIES OF A FAMILY'S GHOSTS IN STONE

DESPITE THE VIKING AND NORMAN elements in its name there is no ancient parish church among the houses in the village of Holme Lacy about 7 miles south-east of Hereford on the road to Fownhope. A lane leads off between fields and shortly passes the gates into the park of a house which has been significant in the history of the area. In another short distance a track leads to the left to end a mile away within a circle of trees adjacent to the church and large churchyard of St Cuthbert. This is the parish church missing from the village. The only other building near by is the former seventeenth-century rectory, exceptionally tall with four storeys. The surrounding land is within a loop of the River

This is a church of the first half of the fourteenth century, whose village was deserted in the later Middle Ages by people escaping from the flooding of the nearby River Wye.

LEFT ABOVE *The south aisle with the nave to the left. The font and benches are seventeenth century and some of the Scudamore monuments are just visible at the east end.*

LEFT BELOW *A misericord on one of the late medieval choir stalls.*

ABOVE LEFT *Monument to John Scudamore (d. 1571) and his wife. Alabaster figures of 'good quality' on a tomb chest with two kneeling angels holding family arms below.*

ABOVE RIGHT *Monument to James Scudamore (d. 1665). His reclining figure gesticulates expressively. Cherubs above prepare to bestow a heavenly garland. The sculptor was possibly Francis Bird, pupil of Grinling Gibbons.*

Wye as it makes its way to Ross-On-Wye and eventually the Severn estuary. The sedges and reeds in the neighbouring fields indicate the regular flooding of the river which is the reason why the original village around the church moved to higher ground in the late Middle Ages. 'Holme' is Old Scandinavian meaning 'island in marshy land'. Medieval villages deserted for one reason or another are frequently the explanation for lonely isolated churches such as this, churches which often nowadays are in the care of the Trust.

After the Norman Conquest the manor was granted to the Bishop of Hereford, who leased it to Roger de Lacey. His family remained here for over 300 years. At the beginning of the fifteenth century they were succeeded as the principal family by the Scudamores from Kentchurch south-west of Hereford. These later became baronets and viscounts who played a major role in county and national life and at the royal court. In the eighteenth century the land passed by marriage to other families and in the nineteenth century it belonged to the Scudamore-Hope family.

There is now no trace of the original Norman church built by Roger de Lacey. The earliest parts of the present church were

ABOVE LEFT *Detail of the monument to Jane Scudamore (d. 1699), wife of James. Baroque decoration at the base of an obelisk.*

ABOVE *Monument to Viscount Sligo (d. 1716). Drapes drawn back reveal two cherubs holding an urn on a sarcophagus within an architectural surround.*

LEFT *Detail of the monument to Viscount Sligo. A skull is a sombre momento mori contrasting sharply with happy cherubs.*

LEFT *Monument to Mary Scudamore Stanhope (d. 1859). Victorian sentimentality has now replaced Baroque theatre.*

RIGHT *Captain Chandos Scudamore Stanhope was drowned on active service in 1871. In another sentimental composition, an angel hovers above an anchor and chain.*

built in 1300–50 of local sandstone, predominantly grey with some dark red. The plan is an unusual one. The nave has one aisle to the south, of the same width and height. As there is no structural division between nave and chancel, and since both nave and aisle have similar plaster tunnel roofs, the effect is of two identical parallel spaces running continuously from east to west. It is a plan more familiar in Welsh and Devon churches. The subdued lighting (there is no clerestory) falling on the dark walls and stone-flagged floor, combined with a lack of clutter, give the interior a cool, dignified atmosphere. The coolness is broken by flashes of rich colour from the stained glass in various parts of the church and the funeral hatchments of the Scudamores. A few of the medieval choir stalls survive.

As would be expected, the church contains many monuments to the family. Such people invariably used their parish church to double as a family mausoleum. The earliest monument is to John Soudamore (d. 1571) and his wife, whose alabaster effigies are 'of very good quality'. On the end of the tomb chest are two kneeling angels and family arms. The Baroque monument to James Scudamore (d. 1668), son of the 1st Lord Scudamore, shows him in Roman costume reclining on a cushion, his right hand gesticulating expressively. Above him, draperies are pulled up to reveal cherubs about to bestow a garland of honour. The composition has typical Baroque theatricality as has the adjacent monument to his wife Jane (d. 1699), where the base of an obelisk is

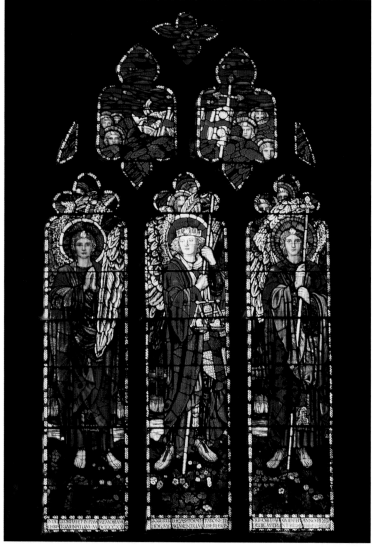

ABOVE LEFT *A collection of small fragments of medieval stained glass brought into one window to create a colourful kaleidoscope. The face of a saint with crown can be seen top left.*

ABOVE RIGHT *Arthurian knights in a memorial window to a soldier killed in the First World War.*

LEFT *Late-seventeenth-century font with the same Baroque decoration seen in the monuments.*

decorated with cherubs heads and draperies. John Scudamore, who was ennobled as Viscout Sligo in 1628 and died in 1671, has a monument as grand as his son's, but without an effigy. Two cherubs hold an urn on top of a sarcophagus within an architectural surround supported by tall fluted Ionic columns. Skulls at the bottom of the sarcophagus are a sombre *memento mori*, contrasting sharply with the prettiness of the cherubs. Grandeur and theatricality give way to sentimentality in the Victorian monuments. Mary Scudamore Stanhope (d. 1859) is commemorated by an female figure of Faith in white marble. The death of Captain Chandos Scudamore-Stanhope occured on active service in 1871 and his monument shows an angel hovering above an anchor and chain.

The late seventeenth century Scudamores contributed other Baroque art to the church in addition to their monuments. The stone font is adorned with the familiar cherubs and swags.

ABOVE LEFT *Gates leading into the Scudamore family's section of the churchyard have the family crest above.*

ABOVE RIGHT *The bronze statue of a medieval knight marks the grave of Edwyn Francis Scudamore-Hope, 10th Earl of Chesterfield (d. 1933).*

BELOW *Holme Lacy House, built in 1695 between the church and the modern village was the former home of the Scudamore family for about 300 years. It is now a country house hotel.*

The best glass in the church by the noted firm of Powell and Sons shows King Arthur and two of his knights to commemorate the bravery of a soldier killed in the First World War. Numerous fragments of medieval glass taken from several windows have been brought together to form a kaleidoscope of colour in a single window. In nineteenth- and twentieth-century restorations this was a common and quite successful way to conserve old pieces that were largely meaningless in isolation.

In the modern era burials are seldom permitted inside parish churches. A section of the churchyard at the east end of the church has been reserved for the Scudamore family. It is entered from outside by wrought-iron gates topped with the family crest. The monument to Edwyn Francis Scudamore-Hope, 10th Earl of Chesterfield (d. 1933) stands out in the form of a bronze sculpture of a medieval soldier. It is unusual to see statues of this kind outside.

The return to the village on the main road will again pass Holme Lacy House, the former home of the Scudamores. It was built in the late seventeenth century, the same time as the principal monuments in the church described above, but compared to them it is 'uncommonly reticent'. Later additions made it the largest house in Herefordshire. The Scudamores departed from Holme Lacy some years ago to return to their original home at Kentchurch. The house is now a country house hotel.

30. ST MARY, LITTLE WASHBOURNE, GLOUCESTERSHIRE

A MARRIAGE OF THE TWELFTH AND EIGHTEENTH CENTURIES

LITTLE WASHBOURNE IS A SCATTERED HAMLET lying under the western escarpment of the Cotswolds close to the Worcestershire border. It is an ancient ecclesiastical site. King Offa of Mercia gave the land to the monks of what is now Worcester Cathedral in AD 780. After various changes in ownership it passed to the Washbourne family in *c.*1250 and they held Great and Little Washbourne until the early nineteenth century.

The little church stands alone in a former apple orchard. It is the simplest two-cell structure of aisleless nave and chancel built in the early twelfth century. Although the original Norman ground plan is preserved, some work

was necessary in the eighteenth century because of concerns about the stability of the building. The heavy diagonal buttresses added on the north, south and east sides are not a visual asset, but the refacing of the walls with ashlar (fine cut) limestone at the same time was done well. The honey-coloured hues of this lovely building stone, seen throughout the Cotswolds, are among the most attractive in England. The doorway and the windows alongside are also eighteenth century. It is strange that they were given pointed Gothic heads. In 1996, the church was roofed with limestone slates, which harmonise well with the masonry below.

ABOVE *The small two-cell church was built in the early twelfth century.*

RIGHT *The walls were resurfaced with finely cut limestone in the eighteenth century and the diagonal buttresses were added for stability. The doorway and windows were given pointed heads at the same time.*

Inside, there is clearer evidence of the Norman origins of the church as well as the overwhelming presence of the eighteenth century. The small round-headed chancel arch has jambs with typical Norman scallop capitals. The Norman window in the north wall of the chancel is deeply splayed to allow of maximum light from the minimum of glazing. The furnishings, however, are completely of the eighteenth century. The tall and handsomely panelled box pews fill the whole of the nave. The two-decker pulpit with tester high above is also panelled and inlaid with lighter wood. This may be a church of the humblest sort, but if the woodwork was introduced by the Washbourne family, it must have involved them in considerable expense. As usual there are simple tiered benches at the back of the church for the labouring class or perhaps for musicians.

The chancel furniture (usually the responsiblity of the rector) is simpler. The altar is a plain table with marble top and the communion rails are equally plain. There is a small decorative wall tablet of 1786.

The fact that the church remained so small throughout the Middle Ages in a prosperous area where most churches were progressively enlarged is explained by its being a chapelry of Overbury Church about 3 miles to the north-west. This is a much larger Norman building with extensive Perpendicular Gothic additions. St Mary's was handed over to the Trust in 1976.

31. CHAPEL OF ST JOHN THE EVANGELIST, CHICHESTER, SUSSEX

PRIVATE ENTERPRISE FOR LOW CHURCH PREACHING

CHICHESTER IS ONE OF THE SMALLEST and most intimate of English cathedral cities. The medieval plan of a main street running north–south crossed by one running east–west is still retained with the city's famous Butter Cross at their intersection in the centre. Close to this is the great Norman cathedral, whose tall spire beckons people to the city for miles around. The chapel of St John The Evangelist in a quiet side street is a few minutes walk away. In its origins, its architecture and former churchmanship it is unique among the Trust's properties.

In the Middle Ages there were six parish churches within the walls of the city, mainly small to serve parishes of only a few hundred people. At the end of the eighteenth century the population of the city had increased to 4,000, and with a high number of churchgoers the seating in the existing churches was seriously inadequate. The building of new churches at this time presented difficulties. Cost was one, ecclesiastical politics was another. Rectors and vicars were reluctant to cede part of their parishes because of the consequent loss of revenue from tithes and the fees for marriages and funerals. The solution was one adopted in several cities from the early eighteenth century: the building of 'proprietary' chapels. Although they were financed privately, often resembled Methodist chapels and followed a very Low Church theology, they were fully within the established Church. A group of wealthy 'shareholders' would provide the money to build the chapel and employ an Anglican clergyman. A return on some of the capital would arise from the outright sale of some of the box pews and a steady income would be obtained from the quarterly rentals of the remainder. The financial interests of the neighbouring clergy were protected because the chapel was extra-parochial, outside the tithe system and weddings and funerals had to be held in the parish church. As a result the buildings were always known as chapels and their incumbents as ministers.

The building of St John's was authorised by an Act of Parliament on 5 May 1812. The Act stipulated that, in addition to the private pews, there should be two 250 free seats for the poor. James Elmes, Surveyor to the nearby cathedral, was appointed architect and the foundation stone was laid on 24 May of the same year. The chapel was consecrated by the Bishop of Chichester on 24 September 1813. The plan is octagonal, and built of white brick which harmonises with the flint of older buildings in the

vicinity. It has no graveyard for the reason mentioned and is set back from the road by only a small courtyard. The details are all Classical as yet unaffected by the dawning of the Gothic Revival movement. Facing the street, a central doorway with pilasters and a plain architrave is flanked by two projecting porches on the adjacent sides of the octagon. There are two tiers of round-headed windows. A triangular gable is set above the central entrance and above that a Portland Stone campanile is a replica of the fourth century BC Choragic Monument to Lysicrates in Athens.

When people enter a church at the west end they generally expect to see an altar directly ahead where the eucharist is celebrated. In St John's Chapel the centre aisle leads down to an extremely high three-decker pulpit, one of the tallest in England. There is no sign of an altar or even a chancel. The pulpit is the focal point of this interior. The lowest deck for the parish clerk and the middle desk for reading the lessons are square. The upper pulpit is circular on a spiral stem resembling a wine glass. The structure is made of American black birch wood. Sermons from this pulpit were seldom less than an hour. The preacher could see all on the ground floor below him and those in the galleries slightly above him. He could also keep an eye on a clock at the front of the west gallery facing him. The visitor has to pass behind the pulpit to see a simple table set against the east wall acting as an altar where, typically, there is no cross or candlesticks. Four panels on the wall behind have

the usual texts of the Commandments, Lord's Prayer and Apostles' Creed.

High galleries run around on all sides supported on slender cast iron columns. All the windows have clear glass. All these features make many visitors assume that this is a nonconformist chapel. Throughout the Victorian period the chapel was under the supervision of extremely Low Church evangelical clergy. We have seen in several places previously that the eighteenth-century Church of England placed more emphasis on prayer and preaching than on the celebration of the eucharist. Not only were the chapel clergy an extreme example of this, they resisted all the blandishments of the High Church Oxford Movement towards a greater emphasis on the sacraments and their associated rituals. St John's is an extraordinary example of the survival into recent times of a form of churchmanship that

OPPOSITE *The entrance front of the octagonal chapel, which was built in 1812. The centre door leads into the ground floor area of free benches. The two side porches lead into ground and upper floor areas of box pews rented or privately owned. A replica of the fourth century* BC *Choragic Monument in Athens above the gable acts as a campanile.*

LEFT *The view from the entrance is not of a chancel and altar but of a tall three-decker pulpit, which is the focal point of the interior. A 'kitchen table' altar is hidden behind against the far wall.*

was already rare at the beginning of the twentieth century.

The chapel retains most of the seating arrangements in their original form. There are three separate areas, reflecting the divisions in the congregation. The centre of the ground floor consists of plain pews facing the pulpit. Since 1879 they have been substantial solid-backed pieces, which replaced simpler open-backed ones installed originally. This area was for the seating of the poor who entered by the central door outside. Under the galleries to the north and south box pews face inwards across the chapel. These were privately owned or rented pews for the wealthier, which were accessed only by the side porches. Thus the two classes of society were in the same room but quite segragated. Anyone committing the faux pas of entering by the wrong door had to leave and re-enter. The galleries above on the north, south and west sides also have box pews, many of which were for 'shareholders' and their families. They are reached by elegantly winding staircases from the side porches. Lines of straight benches behind the box pews were for servants accompanying their employers. The east gallery above the pulpit was for the organ. The original instrument was rebuilt and enlarged many times up to 1950 when it was too worn to repair. What one sees now is a *trompe d'oeil* effect of the front of the organ attached to the east wall.

St John's Chapel was given Grade I listed status in 1950 not because it was outstanding architecture but as a vision of society and church life that lasted continuously throughout the nineteenth century and the first half of the twentieth.

The church builders and administrators had financial difficulties from the start. The musical event at the opening ceremony when distinguished singers were engaged in 1813 lost money. The chapel was closed 1871–4 because of lack of money to pay the minister. Pew rents frequently had to be increased and even those who owned their pews had to meet further charges as their contracts required. In 1955 the maintenance costs and the size of the congregation meant that the chapel had to be amalgamated with the neighbouring parish of St Pancras. From then on it was little used and was declared redundant in 1973. Three years later it passed to the care of the Trust. It is frequently used for concerts and other events.

From the back of the pulpit it is a long climb to the top. It must have taken considerable authority and self-confidence to preach for up to an hour from a pulpit such as this.

32. ST STEPHEN'S OLD CHURCH, FYLINGDALES, NORTH YORKSHIRE

A PLAIN PREACHING BOX ON A NORTHERN MOOR

ABOVE *The view from the churchyard across Robin Hood's Bay. The eponymous fishing village with the spire of New St Stephen's is visible in the middle distance.*

BELOW *The church was built in 1821 on the site of a Norman church demolished the year before. The plain dignified 'preaching box' plan suited the style of Anglican worship at the time. The large churchyard has numerous graves of people lost at sea.*

THE FISHING VILLAGE OF ROBIN HOOD'S BAY is one of many nestling at the bottom of several miles of high cliffs that stretch between Whitby and Scarborough on the Yorkshire coast. In 1966 Nikolaus Pevsner thought that it was 'without question, the most picturesque fishing village of Yorkshire, a maze of little streets and passages with houses on a diversity of levels, some of them with three bay ashlar houses. The village does not recommend itself to cars (the gradient is one in three) and so enjoys the blessings of what planners now call a "pedestrian precinct".' It is just like its counterparts in Cornwall and Devon. There are

two churches associated with the village: St Stephen's Old Church built in 1821, described here, and St Stephen's New Church built in 1870. The old church stands alone about a mile from the village high up behind the cliffs. The new church is down in the village at sea level, a considerable distance away. It might seem strange that the old church was sited where the walk of a mile and a climb of several hundred feet would be an effort for those in the village attending services. However, since the early Middle Ages a church on the site served the village only as part of the large parish of Fylingdales, which covers much of the north-east corner of the North Yorkshire Moors. The site was presumably a compromise to suit the best interests of all. During the nineteenth century, as the village grew in size and the rural population on the moor declined, a new church to provide for the village would have been sensible.

The elevation of St Stephen's Old Church provides extensive views from the churchyard across the fields to the North Sea. A building of 1821 is in fact relatively modern by the standards of English ecclesiology. One can generally assume that a church of this date in a rural situation is a replacement of an older one because the structure of the rural parish system was virtually complete in England by 1200 with only few additions thereafter. The previous church was on the same site but little is known about it except that it was a Norman building and was 'in a way very ruinous and in a decayed state' according to the minister and churchwardens. It may well have had a Saxon predecessor because nearby Whitby was a great ecclesiastical centre in the heroic age of Christianity in Northumbria in the seventh and eighth centuries (pages 26–8). Before the Reformation the advowson (the right to appoint a vicar) and the tithes belonged to St Mary's Abbey at Whitby.

There are striking similarities and equally striking dissimilarities between Chiselhampton church built in 1762 (pages 96–9) and St Stephen's Old Church. Both are rectangular

'preaching boxes' favoured for small churches in the Georgian period. But whereas Chiselhampton externally has a delicate feminine charm with rendered walls and small Classical adornments agreeable to the southern taste, Fylingdales has a stern masculinity deriving from the sombre grey masonry of the local Jurassic sandstone and the lack of any adornments, which give it a character more suited to the northern temperament. It is impossible to imagine Chiselhampton and Fylingdales churches interchanged. St Stephen's is too simple to have an architectural 'style', although the pointed windows are a token nod in the direction of the coming Gothic Revival style that was to dominate the later nineteenth century. There was no architect or building firm involved; contracts were made with a local mason and joiner.

The similarities and dissimilarities between Chiselhampton and Fylingdales continue inside. Both are crammed with box pews arranged around a prominent three-decker pulpit placed against a wall in the middle of the nave. But whereas Chiselhampton is all urbanely polished mahogany, Fylingdales is all pinewood painted in two shades of grey, a rustic but attractive choice. There is a contrast too in chancels. Chiselhampton has a handsome carved reredos covering the whole of the east wall behind the altar; Fylingdales has only a simple altar table placed below the east window. Both churches have large clear glass windows which flood the interiors with light. Apart from the differences in southern and northern tastes the contrasts between the two churches relate to the differences in patrons and finance. Chiselhampton was initiated and financed by a wealthy landowner who was prepared to go to considerable (but not extravagant) expense whereas the building of Fylingdales was initiated by two churchwardens who organised door-to-door collections in the parish and solicited donations from all over the north-east.

The three-decker pulpit is impressively tall and wide and the benches in the pews are designed to face it. As usual at this time, the box pews for the gentry and wealthier farmers at the front of the church are taller than those behind to emphasise the stratification of society in early-nineteenth-century England. A dog-legged gallery built on the west and north sides carries forward right up to the chancel. The size of the regular congregation that this implies is astonishing considering the distances that people had to travel on horse or on foot to this isolated building. The organ frame in the west gallery is the remains of an old barrel type of instrument. Other musicians sat in the gallery facing the pulpit. There are notches still to be seen at the edge of the pews which held the music stands for the string and reed instruments of the time. An old Victorian stove and flue are still in place beneath the gallery.

The church and the parish have naturally had a long association with the sea and seamen. There is a large model of the SS *Pretoria* kept in a glass case in the nave. A book completed in 1912 records the names of 260 seamen of the parish who from 1686 lost their lives at sea either drowned in shipwrecks or killed in naval battles. The large churchyard contains scores of graves referring to such losses. A local schoolmistress composed several of the inscriptions.

> By storms at sea two sons I lost
>   which sore distressed me
> Because I can not have their bones
>   to anchor here with me.

When the moorland church replaced the old Norman building in 1821, it was for a time the 'new' church until 1870 when it in turn became the 'old' church that it is today. When New St Stephen's was opened down in the village Old St Stephen's was inevitably used less frequently, usually for burial services. In the early twentieth century at least one vicar attempted to use it more regularly on Sundays but it must have been a losing battle throughout the rest of the twentieth century. The church was handed over to the Trust in 1975.

A model of SS Pretoria in the nave is appropriate in a church closely associated with the sea and seamen for centuries.

33. THE MILTON MAUSOLEUM, MARKHAM CLINTON, NOTTINGHAMSHIRE

PARISH CHURCH APPENDED TO A DUCHESS'S CATACOMB

THE DUKES OF NEWCASTLE came into possession of the vast Clumber estate at the northern end of Sherwood Forest in the early eighteenth century. This was in addition to the neighbouring estate of Welbeck Abbey which their ancestors acquired after the Dissolution of the monasteries in the 1530s. The house that was first built at Clumber 1760–70 was greatly enlarged in stages in the nineteenth century. Except for a small fragment it was demolished in 1938 when even the very wealthy were beginning to find such seats unaffordable.

The estate, which covers some 20 square miles, is now managed by the National Trust for public use. Several entrances lead into a maze of driveways which wend their way around lakes and through woodlands, shrubberies and open grassland. It is a paradise for walkers and cyclists.

1822 was a tragic year for the 4th Duke. His eldest daughter died early in in the year. His wife Georgiana died giving birth to twins on 26 September when a girl was stillborn and a boy survived just ten days. Duke and Duchess were

The church from the entrance to the churchyard. It is actually two buildings in one. The parish church is to the west (left), entered by the small doorway in the west wall. The transepts with crossing tower and octogon above and everything to the east (right) is the private mausoleum. It was completed in 1827.

The east end is the private entrance for visiting members of the Duke's family. The giant portico has four Greek Doric columns.

particularly attached and he planned at first to build a special extension of the family vault in the parish church at Bothamsall, one of the nearest villages to the house in the park, to accommodate her and the children. Sir Robert Smirke, architect of the British Museum, was commissioned to design the building. Before this was begun it was decided to change the site to West Markham parish church about 3 miles further away. The Duke wrote: 'I took Mr Smirke to West Markham where there is a very bad church and I mean to move it to a more central position.' The nearby hamlet of Clinton was chosen for this new mausoleum-cum-church but the 'very bad' church at West Markham was not in the event demolished.

The mausoleum – it was essentially that because the parish church element must always have been of minor consequence to the Duke – was started in 1824 and apart from the adjacent rectory provided by the Duke stands alone among the fields. It is a large church, built of Roche Abbey stone from South Yorkshire, a strikingly white magnesian limestone (see Lead, pages 132–4). From the churchyard entrance at the west end the church appears to consist of nave, transepts and chancel, with a low squat crossing tower surmounted by an octagon with a cupola above. Everything is severely plain in a Neoclassical way. This view suggests a traditionally planned interior which is misleading because there are two separate buildings within. An inspection of the whole exterior gives a clear clue. The west end has a doorway into the nave in the traditional place, although it is smaller and plainer than would be expected in a building of this size. A walk through long grass round to the east end reveals not the expected plain wall and window lighting the chancel, but the very unexpected sight of a giant Greek Doric portico with four columns approached by steps. This appears to be the main entrance to a church oriented back to front. However, no ordinary parishioners entered here, theirs was the small doorway at the west end. This grand eastern entrance was for the Duke's family visiting the mausoleum part of the building.

The overall effect of all this is highly incongruous. The Roche Abbey limestone resembles Portland stone, so this might be one of the churches built in the City of London in the late eighteenth or early nineteenth century, or as Pevsner remarks in one of the outlying boroughs of Hackney or Wandsworth. Christopher Wren had popularised the use of the stone a century earlier but there are no surrounding City offices or suburban houses here, only the adjacent rectory and Nottinghamshire fields. The Classical grandeur too seems incongruous in such a setting.

The division of the interior into two entirely separate parts is immediately evident on entering. The small west door leads into an aisleless nave which terminates in a cross-wall cutting off the transepts and everything further east. The lower part of this is concealed by a heavy oak reredos with six fluted Ionic columns. The altar that once stood at the centre has been removed. Most of the box pews that once filled the nave have also been removed. Those that remain are painted in blue and white, a not unattractive if unusual choice.

Openings at the ends of the reredos lead into a passage between it and the cross-wall and from that there is a doorway into the mausoleum beneath the octagon and cupola which lights it. To the left and right the transepts contain the family's memorials at ground level but not the actual burials. First in importance is that of Georgiana, the 4th Duke's wife. She sits on a bed holding her infant twins who died with her. Behind them a hovering figure incorporates the death mask of the daughter who died before them earlier the same year. Her husband the Duke died in 1851 and his monument is near by. Interestingly, although the Duchess's monument is in the Classical style prevalent in the 1820s, his is in the Gothic Revival style which had gained acceptance in the intervening years. Two page boys in medieval dress stand with respectfully bowed heads in front of a reredos with a foiled

ogee arch. There is no effigy of the Duke himself. Surprisingly, the actual entombment section of the mausoleum is beneath the parishioners' nave. In front of the altar there are two rings in a flagstone. This was lifted by machinery (the churchwardens were paid) when a coffin was to be lowered into the vault below. We can imagine the funeral of the Duchess: the grieving family grouped around a coffin disappearing from view, the men in wide-legged trousers holding stovepipe hats, the women in long black dresses and veiled. The vault below is 66 feet long and 17 feet wide. The side walls are divided into recesses six and three high on each side – thirty-six recesses in all. With each holding two coffins, there is space for seventy-two people. The vault was permanently bricked up in 1980, following a break-in by thieves who believed wrongly a local legend that Georgiana had been buried in her state jewels.

In 1949 the then Duke of Newcastle indicated that the family could no longer support the church

The nave from the west end. Behind the reredos it is closed off by a cross-wall. A doorway behind the reredos leads into the mausoleum beyond. Only a few of the original painted box pews remain in the nave.

and the parishioners took a vote on whether to continue using this 'new' church at Milton or return to the old church at West Markham. They chose the old church. From the very beginning, the parishioners of the 1820s could surely have never liked this church, which aristocratic power had unilaterally imposed upon them. In the new church there must always have been the feeling of worshipping in the appendage to a mausoleum. As a result of the decision of the parishioners the church/mausoleum was handed over to the Trust in 1972.

The 4th Duke seems to have had a premonition of what was to happen. After looking round the newly built church, before it was consecrated he wrote in his diary: 'I could not help reflecting upon the futility of all human arangements. Nor mindful that my forecast might be useless, for families more numerous than mine have been swept away even before manhood.' How many of those seventy-two places in the vault were ever filled? And did he foresee that nothing would survive of a palatial house at Clumber except for a stable block? And there is a footnote to add about 'the futility of human arrangements'. On the road outside the churchyard there is a short length of Lombardy poplars on either side. It was intended that these would stretch back as an avenue all the way to Clumber, connecting Georgiana's home with her tomb, but the project was never completed. The atmosphere at Milton is for obvious reasons more ghostly than at most Trust churches. Now even the pathway leading up to the grand eastern portico has disappeared under the long grass.

In the south transept within the mausoleum section there are two memorials. Left: Duchess Georgiana, for whom the whole building was erected, sits on a bed with her infant twins who died with her in childbirth in 1822. Behind them the hovering figure incorporates the death mask of another daughter who died earlier in the same year. Right: Georgiana's husband, the 4th Duke, died in 1851. By that time the Gothic Revival style had replaced the Classical, as shown by the ogee arch on the reredos. Two pageboys in medieval dress stand with respectfully bowed heads.

34. ST GREGORY, SEDBERGH, VALE OF LUNE, CUMBRIA

A STRANGE BY-PRODUCT OF VICTORIAN RAILWAY CONSTRUCTION

If st gregory's church were listed in a catalogue of second-hand books it might be listed under 'Curiosa'. Everything about it is curious: its situation, its history and its furnishings. Many motorists will come here via the M6 motorway where the Kendal (west) and Sedbergh (east) exit is only about 3 miles away. This is the spot where the motorway, after climbing gradually from Lancaster, has reached one of its highest points before descending in sweeeping curves to Tebay between high, unfenced fells on either side. The rollercoaster road to Sedbergh passes through scenery that is an attractive hybrid of farmland and fell, where moss- and fern-covered rocks outcrop among the fields. It crosses the River Lune shortly before the church.

St Gregory's is about 2 miles west of the little market town of Sedbergh. Although it stands alongside the road, it is easy to miss because it is tucked in between two cottages of the same height so can easily be mistaken for a barn or byre when passing in a car. There are no other buildings in sight. It is not unusual to see Methodist chapels isolated on roadsides like this; it is less common to see an Anglican church. In 1860, large numbers of navvies were engaged in the area building a branch railway line from Ingleton in West Yorkshire to Penrith, where it would join the main line to Scotland. The railway company employed a Scripture Reader, a Mr Foyers, to minister to its workers. He had done similar work successfully

TOP *The 'plain and simple' church of 1860 is on a roadside among the Cumbrian fells with two cottages as close neighbours.*

ABOVE *The interior was refurnished in 1900 by local carpenters using wood from local oaks.*

LEFT *Four of the unusual stained-glass windows showing local scenery, flora and fauna. It has an Arts and Crafts quality, typical of 1900.*

ABOVE *A porch window by the firm of Morris and Co. shows an angel as a symbol of peace.*

elsewhere and his ministry here proved equally popular not only with the navvies but also with the local farmers. When the line was completed and the workers had left, Mr Foyers was ready to follow them until the farmers petitioned Miss Frances Upton of Ingmere Hall about half a mile away to provide a small church where he could continue his ministry. She agreed to a 'plain and simple' structure and work started in the early 1860s on a building in which church, Hall and schoolroom were combined. It was a T-shaped building of Westmorland slate: stone for the walls, tiles for the roof. It is well lit by windows in the south and west sides and by a gallery of windows set in a vertical roof extension.

In 1900 it was decided to convert the building into a church only. Miss Upton's sister, Mrs Florence Cottrell-Dormer, was responsible for installing new furnishings of considerable quality, probably made by Ingmere Hall estate carpenters using wood from local oak trees. The lower half of the walls was panelled and a set of sturdy benches, inserted in the nave. The altar and reredos were copied from one that

Mrs Cottrell-Dormer had seen elsewhere in the county, its design influenced by the then current Arts and Crafts style. What principally catches the eye around the whole church, however, is a set of stained-glass windows made by a London firm, Campbell, Smith and Co. These too were influenced by Arts and Crafts, and F.G. Smith, who designed the pictures, seems to have had some knowledge of the surrounding countryside. The windows show local scenery, rivers, trees, plants and birds in rich glowing colours. The professional art world may think little of work like this but it probably charms the majority of ordinary visitors today. As church windows they are unusual in having no overt religious content, pointing instead to God through His natural creation in the outside world. In contrast, two windows in the chancel are by the firm of Morris and Co. (Morris himself had died in 1896). A window in the porch, an ever-popular angel figure, is also said to be one of theirs.

In 1917, the Upton family transferred ownership of the church to the Church Commissioners and it was consecrated for the Church of England by the Bishop of Richmond in 1918. The dedication to St Gregory the Great dates from this time. The church was declared redundant in 1992 and vested in the Trust. The railway line which created the church was closed to passenger traffic in 1954 (well before Dr Beeching's onslaught) and later dismantled. The numerous narrow lanes in the area are constantly crossing over or under the course of the former lines by means of little sandstone bridges, witness to the immense efforts of those navvies 150 years ago. After leaving the church visitors can pause at the churchyard gate to take in the magnificent view and perhaps to wander among these lanes.

The magnificent view from the churchyard gate. These fells lie on the border between Cumbria and North Yorkshire.

35. CHRIST THE CONSOLER, SKELTON-CUM-NEWBY, NORTH YORKSHIRE

A NOBLEWOMAN'S MEMORIAL TO A MURDERED SON

THE VILLAGE OF SKELTON is about 4 miles east of Ripon, insulated from some of the noise and pace of modern life by a few miles of country lanes. Its single street of mainly eighteenth- and early-nineteenth-century stone and brick houses ends at two tall gates impressively guarded on either side by a square turret and linked lodge. A long, straight driveway beyond leads to Newby Hall, hidden away in its extensive grounds. The village and the Hall have had a close relationship for several centuries.

The Hall was built originally in 1705 by Sir Frances Blackett, whose wealth came from coal

BELOW *The church was built in 1871–6 in the High Victorian Gothic Revival style. The east end is seen here in early spring, before it was screened by the large weeping beeches in leaf.*

RIGHT *Eighteenth-century Newby Hall, the home of Lady Mary Vyner, who built the church within the grounds.*

RIGHT BELOW *The south-west view from the park of Newby Hall.*

mining in the Newcastle area. Blackett's mansion was a single rectangular Classical block of red brick with stone dressings. In 1748 the house was sold to Richard Weddell, whose son William was a notable connoiseur of architecture and art. He employed the leading Neoclassical architect Robert Adam to add two side wings to the central block and to provide interiors throughout, the design and decorative plasterwork of which are 'among the finest of their kind in Europe'. Adam also designed the grand entrance to the park referred to above. After Weddell's death in 1792, the property went to his cousin Thomas Robinson, 3rd Lord Grantham, and from him to his daughter Lady Mary Robinson (1809–92), who became Lady Mary Vyner on her marriage to Henry Vyner. It is with her that the story of the church begins. In 1870, her twenty-three-year-old son Frederick was travelling with seven companions in Greece when they were captured by brigands who demanded a ransom of £32,000 (the equivalent of some two million pounds today). The money was dispatched but during a botched rescue attempt by Greek soldiers Frederick was killed by the brigands and the ransom was never handed over. At this time the parish church of Skelton and Newby Hall was a small eighteenth-century stone building in the village street, looking more like a Methodist chapel than a traditional Anglican church. After Frederick's death the grieving and pious mother decided to build a new church with the unused ransom money. It was decided that the new church would be within the grounds of the Hall, leaving the old church in position. The new church bears no relationship, however, to the sort of churches at Gunton, Norfolk (pages 104–7), Nuneham Courtenay, Oxfordshire (pages 108–12) or Croome d'Abitot, Worcestershire (pages 113–19), which were built as architectural ornaments within landscaped parks for the visual enjoyment of the owners and their guests, with little regard for religion or the convenience of the villagers. Lady Vyner's church at Skelton was built from genuine Christian feeling and for the benefit of all the local community.

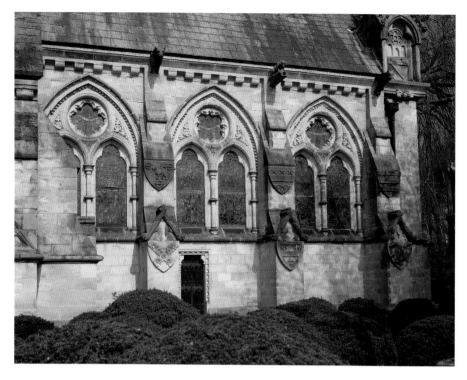

TOP *The chancel retains the medieval custom of having a priest's door. All the Gothic Revival details of the exterior, however, are more boldly assertive than their medieval models.*

ABOVE *The organist's seat is placed on a corbel carved with grotesque animals.*

RIGHT *The great height of the interior derives from French medieval Gothic. Note the subsidiary shafts of Irish black marble on the piers, contrasting with the white marble sculpture of the Ascension of Christ high above the chancel arch. The organ occupies a prominent position high up at the junction of nave and chancel.*

Accordingly it was sited in a corner of the park immediately adjacent to the village street, which would involve a walk of only a few hundred yards for these attending services. In fact, church and Hall are not visible from each other, although the tower of the church, visible over the surrounding trees from the driveway to the Hall would have been a constant reminder of Frederick to Lady Vyner, and no doubt a constant consolation to her when leaving and returning home. Hence the dedication to Christ the Consoler.

To design the church Lady Vyner chose William Burges (1827–81), one of the leading architects of the High Victorian period. He favoured the most flamboyant forms of the Gothic Revival style particularly in the way of interior decoration. In this he was influenced by the work of the father of Gothic Revival architecture A.W.N. Pugin (1812–52) taking it to new heights of opulence. Burges probably came to the notice of Lady Vyner through a family connection with the 3rd Marquess of Bute, owner of Cardiff Castle, where Burges designed the richest of Victorian interiors, dazzling in their polychromatic materials and unusual forms. The church is approached from the village street through a wicket gate close to Robert Adam's entrance to the park. For 100 yards a footpath leads beneath a canopy of conifers, which opens up suddenly to reveal the church a similar distance away, surrounded only by huge weeping trees, fields and grazing sheep. It consists of chancel, aisled nave and a steeple asymmetrically placed on the north side. The style is the Decorated form Gothic, the favourite of the Victorians in these years. There is no mistaking the typically bold, assertive massing of parts characteristic of the mid-nineteenth century. The decorative details follow medieval Gothic forms, but they too are equally assertively stressed. The material is buff sandstone throughout, well chosen for its durable quality.

An ornate porch and heavy oak doors, with much decorative wrought ironwork, lead inside. The interior is impressively high in the French

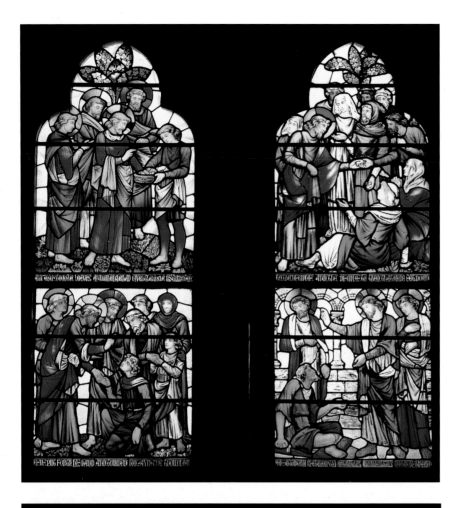

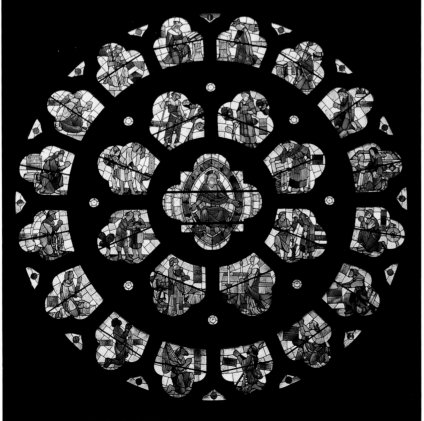

Gothic manner, which Burges absorbed while studying and working in France. Two things make the architecture memorable: the design of secondary features within a conventional overall plan, and the spectacular use of coloured materials. Secondary features include the subsidiary shafts to the main arcade piers and the use of shafts and open unglazed tracery in front of all the windows in aisles, clerestory and chancel. As regards materials, Burges switched from the rather dour sandstone without to a creamy limestone for the essential structure of walls and piers. This is embellished by a variety of handsome polychromatic marbles, which make the building a geologist's paradise. The subsidiary detached shafts of the piers are a jet black Irish marble. The choice of this unusual stone may be linked in this memorial church to the Victorian love of the visible signs of mourning. Any overall sense of gloom is dispelled, however, by the use of white marble for the prominent sculpture of the Ascension of Christ watched by the apostles, positioned high above the chancel arch. Gloom is also dispelled by the richness of the stained glass used throughout the building. Its glowing but not strident colours and clarity of design are superior to most Victorian work. It was obviously influenced by the contemporary Arts and Crafts glass of William Morris and Edward Burne-Jones. The themes of much of the glass are the miracles of Christ in curing the sick and afflicted. The rose window, which fills the upper part of the west wall, is a typically French feature. The organ is prominent, high up at the junction

LEFT ABOVE *One of the vibrantly colourful stained-glass windows. Many of them take the theme of Christ the Conosoler as He works miracles to help the sick and needy. Above, left and right: the miracle of the loves and fishes. Below left: 'Be thou healed'. Below right: 'Take up thy bed and walk'.*

LEFT BELOW *The rose window at the west end of the nave is characteristic of French Gothic.*

RIGHT *The organ and organists's balcony seat seen from the chancel.*

The lower section of the wooden font canopy shows the Baptism of Christ by St John the Baptist.

The north-east corner of the chancel. The windows throughout the church have an inner screen of shafts and open tracery.

of nave and chancel. The organist's seat is on a corbel carved with grotesque animals. At the west end the sides of the font are covered with mosaics and the lower part of its tall wooden canopy has a carving of the baptism of Christ by John the Baptist.

The chancel is, if anything, richer again than the nave. The subsidiary shafts on piers now appear in pink, red and green marbles and there is horizontal banding in the same materials. The altar has a reredos with figure work and mosaics. The choir stalls have carved ends. The 'soft furnishings' have the same opulence as the stonework. The original altar frontal designed by Lady Vyner is still in position.

Descendants of the Vyner family still live at Newby Hall, which is open to the public from Easter to autumn. The church is open daily on an independent basis without charge. A combined visit to both is a multi-faceted experience, involving eighteenth-century Neoclassical secular architecture and

art surrounded by idyllic pleasure gardens together with nineteenth-century religious Gothic Revival architecture and art in a pastoral parkland setting. These are a remarkable combination of the English visual arts at their best, but one may recall the statement of the architect W.D. Caröe quoted in the final paragraph of the Introduction. He regarded the glory of a building as 'the deep sense of voicefulness which we feel in walls which have long been washed by passing waves of humanity'. Newby church is deeply imbued with the voice of just one particular lady afflicted with an especially tragic bereavement. This combination of human emotion with architecture and art makes a visit to the church a uniquely memorable experience, and as good a place as any to end these thirty-six journeys across England – journeys which have revealed something of the extent and variety of the Trust's work and its importance for present and future generations.

The extensive use of coloured marbles in the chancel gives this area a sense of special opulence.

TOP *Orange, red and green marbles together with local sandstone in the shafts of the piers.*

ABOVE *The same stones in a frieze running above the choir stalls incorporate the family arms.*

TOP *An angel musician on the end of a choir stall.*

ABOVE *A detail of the original altar frontal designed by Lady Mary Vyner reflects the opulence of the whole interior.*

MAP OF THE CHURCHES

CORNWALL
7. St Anthony, St Anthony-in-Roseland

CUMBRIA
16. St Ninian, Brougham
34. St Gregory, Sedbergh, Vale of Lune

DEVON
25. St Petrock, Parracombe

DORSET
2. St Andrew, Winterborne Tomson

GLOUCESTERSHIRE
30. St Mary, Little Washbourne

GREATER MANCHESTER
17. St Werburgh Old Church, Warburton

HEREFORDSHIRE
28. St Bartholomew, Richard's Castle
29. St Cuthbert, Holme Lacy

KENT
9. All Saints, West Stourmouth

LANCASHIRE
18. St John the Baptist Old Church, Pilling

LEICESTERSHIRE
15. Withcote Chapel
24. All Saints, Stapleford

LINCOLNSHIRE
11. All Saints, Theddlethorpe All Saints

NORFOLK
3. St Margaret, Hales, and St Gregory, Heckingham
6. St Mary, West Walton
14. St Mary, Wiggenhall St Mary
21. St Andrew, Gunton

NORTHAMPTONSHIRE
5. St Peter, Northampton

NORTHUMBERLAND
1. St Andrew, Bywell
20. St Andrew, Shotley

NORTH YORKSHIRE
10. Holy Trinity, Goodramgate, York
26. St Mary, Lead
32. St Stephen Old Church, Fylingdales
35. Christ the Consoler, Skelton-cum-Newby

NOTTINGHAMSHIRE
33. The Milton Mausoleum, Markham Clinton

OXFORDSHIRE
19. St Katherine, Chiselhampton
22. All Saints Old Church, Nuneham Courtenay

SHROPSHIRE
4. St Michael, Upton Cressett

SUFFOLK
12. St Mary, Badley

SUSSEX
31. St John the Evangelist, Chichester

WILTSHIRE
8. St John the Baptist, Inglesham
27. St Mary, Old Dilton

WORCESTERSHIRE
13. St Lawrence, Evesham
23. St Mary Magdalene, Croome d'Abitot

Discover over 340 beautiful churches in the care of the Churches Conservation Trust at visitchurches.org.uk

NORTH
ATLANTIC
OCEAN

SCOTLAND

NORTH
SEA

NORTHERN
IRELAND

IRISH
SEA

Bywell
01
20
Shotley

16
Brougham

34
Vale of Lune

32
Fylingdales

35 Skelton-cum-Newby

10 Goodramgate

18
Pilling

26
Lead

REPUBLIC
OF IRELAND

17
Warburton

West Markham
33

11
Theddlethorpe
All Saints

ENGLAND

Stapleford

Wiggenhall
St Mary
21 Gunton

Upton Cresset
04

24

06
West Walton

14

03
Heckingham

WALES

28 Richard's Castle

15
Withcote

05
Northampton

12
Badley

Croome d'Abitot **23**
13
Evesham

Holme Lacy **29**

30
Little Washbourne

19 Chiselhampton

08
Inglesham

22 Nuneham Courtenay

09
West Stourmouth

25
Parracombe

27
Old Dilton

Chichester
31

Parracombe

CELTIC
SEA

02
Winterborne
Tomson

07
St Anthony-in-Roseland